LGBTQ+ PARENTS GUIDE TO RAISING KIDS WITH PRIDE

Exploring Pathways to Parenthood and Implementing Parenting Strategies to Overcome Challenges and Build Inclusive Lives

ALEX HARPER

Contents

Introduction

In the heart of a bustling city park, amidst the laughter of children and the distant bark of dogs, two dads chase a toddler who is gleefully defying the laws of gravity and toddlerhood. Nearby, two moms share a quiet moment, their newborn asleep against a chest. Each family, unique in their makeup, is bound by a common thread—love. This is the essence of '*LGBTQ+ Parents Guide to Raising Kids With Pride.*' This book is your guide, ally, and companion in the journey of LGBTQ+ parenting, where every family narrative is as unique as the love that defines it.

As an author, my journey into the heart of LGBTQ+ parenting advocacy began when I saw firsthand the lack of resources that spoke directly to our families' intricacies and beauty. With a background in social advocacy and being an ally to the LGBTQ+ community, I've experienced and witnessed the thirst for knowledge, support, and recognition. This book is a response to that need—a comprehensive guide designed to empower you, whether you are a parent, a prospective parent, or an ally.

'*LGBTQ+ Parents Guide to Raising Kids With Pride*' delves into the legal, social, and emotional landscapes that shape your parenting experience. From adoption and surrogacy to biological parenting and foster care, this book covers a spectrum of pathways to parenthood, paired with practical advice and legal insights. It's structured to provide stories, guidance, and tools—checklists, legal toolkits, and directories—that you can apply directly to your life.

You, as LGBTQ+ parents and prospective parents, are the heart of this book's readership. It speaks to your experiences, challenges, and joys. Allies, too, will find this book invaluable for understanding how to support LGBTQ+ families in their communities effectively. Together, we are paving the way for a future where all family structures are recognized and celebrated.

Within these pages, you'll find a variety of family stories, including those from single LGBTQ+ parents, polyamorous families, and trans and non-binary parents. These narratives are crucial, providing representation and practical advice grounded in lived experiences. They serve as a testament to the resilience and diversity of our community.

This guide is crafted to be both a source of comfort and a practical tool. It offers up-to-date legal information, mental health resources, and actionable advice to navigate the complexities of LGBTQ+ parenting. Additionally, it invites you to engage with a broader community, fostering connections and discussions that extend beyond the book.

As we turn the page, let us hold onto the message of empowerment, belonging, and joy. '*LGBTQ+ Parents Guide to Raising Kids With Pride*' is more than a guide—it is a celebration of our families, a tool for advocacy, and a source of hope for current and future LGBTQ+ parents. Together, let's cherish and champion the diversity of family life, ensuring that every narrative is heard and every family feels at home in the world they help to shape.

ONE

Setting the Foundation

As you step into parenting within the LGBTQ+ community, think of this chapter as your trusty map, guiding you through the complex paths of choices and challenges that may lie ahead. It's not just about finding a route to parenthood; it's about choosing the path that resonates with your values, lifestyle, and dreams. Whether you're contemplating adoption, intrigued by surrogacy, considering biological parenting through IVF or IUI, or looking into fostering, each avenue comes with its unique set of challenges to navigate.

Remember, there's no one-size-fits-all approach here. Just as every family is unique, so is every journey to parenthood. What works splendidly for one family might be a better fit for another. It's all about finding the right balance that feels like home to you. So, let's explore these options together, armed with stories from those who've walked these paths before and equipped with the knowledge to make informed decisions that pave the way for your future family.

Choosing the Right Path: Family Building Options

When it comes to building a family, the options available to you as LTBTQ+ individuals are as diverse and varied as our community itself. Each method—adoption, surrogacy, IVF, and fostering—has its benefits and challenges suited to different needs and situations.

Adoption offers a profound opportunity to provide a loving home to a needy child. Many find this path rewarding in the joy of parenting and the knowledge of giving a child a new start. However, it's important to be aware of the legal intricacies, which can vary wildly from one jurisdiction to another, and the potential for emotionally charged processes, including dealing with birth parents and the adoption system.

Surrogacy provides a means to have a biological connection to your child, which, for many, is a deeply held desire. It involves a surrogate mother carrying your child, an option that has grown in popularity and acceptance. Yet, it's accompanied by considerable financial costs and, often, complex legal agreements, making it crucial to have clear contracts and understandings from the outset.

In Vitro Fertilization (IVF) and Intrauterine Insemination (IUI) are medical procedures that allow you to have a child biologically related to you or your partner. IVF involves the fertilization of an egg outside the body and its subsequent implantation into the uterus, while IUI involves the direct insertion of sperm into the uterus. Both options require a significant emotional and financial commitment and, often, a journey through hormonal treatments and medical interventions.

Fostering is another path where you can provide temporary or permanent care to children who may eventually return to their birth families or become a permanent part of yours. It's a path filled with uncertainties but also immense rewards as you directly impact a child's life in their time of need.

Countless individuals in our community walk each path, each with their own stories of challenges and triumphs. Take, for example, Bailey and Jordan, who chose surrogacy and faced a daunting array of legal hurdles and societal misconceptions but ultimately found the process incredibly fulfilling as they welcomed their daughter Mia. Or consider Jamie, who adopted her son, Noah, navigating the complexities of the adoption system and finding joy in the unexpected support of a network of fellow adoptive parents.

When deciding which path might be right for you, consider factors such as your values—do you feel a strong desire for a biological connection to your child? Your health—what medical interventions are you comfortable with? How might Your age affect your choice and experience in the adoption process or through biological methods? And, of course, your financial situation—what are you able to invest in the process of building your family?

Numerous resources can offer support and in-depth information for those exploring these options. Websites like the Human Rights Campaign (HRC) provide detailed guides on LGBTQ+ adoption and surrogacy laws. Books like "The Ultimate Guide for Gay Dads" and "Confessions of the Other

Mother" offer personal insights and practical advice on various aspects of LGBTQ+ parenting. Moreover, LGBTQ+ friendly agencies such as the Family Equality Council offer workshops and seminars that can provide valuable guidance and networking opportunities.

Interactive Element: Family-Building Path Quiz

Consider taking this brief quiz to help you make a decision that best suits your unique situation. Your answers about personal preferences, lifestyle, and values will suggest a family-building path. This tool is intended to guide your thoughts and help you reflect on what option might feel most aligned with your dreams of parenthood.

As you mull over these options, remember there's no rush. Take the time you need to weigh the pros and cons, talk with partners, friends, or counselors, and reach out to community networks. After all, this is about your family, future, and journey to parenthood.

Legal Primer for Prospective LGBTQ+ Parents

Navigating the legal side of LGBTQ+ parenthood can be confusing and challenging, with new issues popping up just when you think you've got it figured out. But fear not! Understanding the basic legal rules and being well-prepared can clarify this confusing process. Let's start with the legal frameworks governing biological, adoptive, and foster parenting. Each of these paths has distinct legal nuances. For biological parenting, legal considerations often revolve around genetic connections and the rights of donors if involved. Adoptive parenting, meanwhile, requires navigating the legal processes of terminating the rights of biological parents and establishing your own. Foster parenting can be even more complex legally, involving state agencies and temporary caregiving rights that may or may not lead to adoption.

Imagine planning a family vacation, but each state you travel through has different traffic laws. Similarly, state and country laws vary significantly regarding LGBTQ+ parenting. Some regions offer robust protections and recognition for LGBTQ+ families, while others may present hurdles such as prohibitions on adoption or ambiguities in parental rights. This patchwork of laws isn't just confusing—it can directly impact your parenting experience. For instance, some states allow for second-parent adoptions, granting legal rights to a non-biological parent, while others do not. Being well-informed about the laws in your area or any area you might consider moving to is crucial.

Legal challenges can be daunting, especially in areas with less progressive laws. Here's where a strategic approach comes into play. First, consider connecting with legal professionals who specialize in LGBTQ+ family law. They can provide guidance tailored to your specific circumstances. Additionally, joining local or national advocacy groups can offer support and resources. These organizations often have experience navigating discrimination and can offer both legal advice and emotional support. For example, if you encounter resistance while securing parental rights, these groups can help you advocate for your family.

Lastly, let's talk about paperwork. It's about as exciting as watching paint dry, but just as a well-painted wall protects your house, thorough legal preparation protects your family.

Essential documents might include wills, which ensure your assets are distributed according to your wishes; medical directives, which outline your healthcare preferences; and second-parent adoption papers, crucial for non-biological parents to establish legal parentage. Imagine you're building a safety net, thread by thread, with each document adding a layer of security for your family's future.

By combining knowledge, preparation, and proactive strategies, you can navigate the legal intricacies of LGBTQ+ parenting with greater confidence and clarity. Whether you're just starting to consider parenthood or are already on your path, understanding and addressing these legal aspects is vital in safeguarding your family's rights and well-being.

How to Secure Legal Parental Status

Imagine holding your child for the first time, the emotional cocktail of joy, awe, and a smidge of terror. Now, imagine feeling a shadow of uncertainty over this moment because your legal relationship with this child isn't yet secure. This is a reality for many LGBTQ+ parents, underscoring why securing legal parental status isn't just a bureaucratic formality—it's a crucial step in affirming and protecting your relationship with your child. Legal parental status solidifies your rights and responsibilities towards your child, including custody, care, and decision-making. It ensures that you can make medical decisions, handle educational matters, and be there legally for your child through thick and thin.

Securing this status can vary greatly depending on your path to parenthood. For those who adopt, parental rights are typically established through adoption, which legally recognizes you as the child's parent. Biological parents, on the other hand, often have parental rights established at birth. Still, for LGBTQ+ parents, especially those who use methods like surrogacy or IVF, the process might involve additional legal steps such as pre-birth orders or post-birth second-parent adoptions. In cases of surrogacy, for instance, intended parents must usually work with legal representatives to ensure their names are on the birth certificate, sometimes requiring court orders depending on state laws.

Consider the case of Erin and Riley, a lesbian couple who used a sperm donor to conceive. Erin carried the baby and thus was automatically recognized as a mother. However, for Riley to gain legal recognition as the other parent, they had to go through a second-parent adoption process involving home visits, heaps of paperwork, and a series of court appearances. Despite the hurdles, securing this legal recognition was paramount, ensuring both were legally acknowledged as parents and safeguarding their family unit.

Then there's advocacy and its transformative role in enhancing LGBTQ+ parental rights. Engaging in advocacy isn't just about attending rallies; it's about understanding the laws, knowing your rights, and being prepared to stand up for them. It's also about collective action, working alongside organizations that fight for LGBTQ+ rights, and helping to push for legal changes that make pathways to parenthood less cumbersome and more inclusive. Take, for instance, the recent changes in several states where laws have been amended to simplify the process for LGBTQ+ individuals to secure parental rights, largely due to persistent advocacy efforts by community members and allies. These changes improve individual lives and set precedents that benefit broader community rights.

Engaging in this advocacy means staying informed about local and national laws, joining and supporting LGBTQ+ advocacy groups, and even reaching out to legislators about the importance of inclusive and equitable parental rights laws. It's about using your voice, whether in person, via blogs, social media, or community forums, to share your experiences and rally for change. Every story told, and every voice raised contributes to a growing chorus that can shift public perception and policy alike.

Navigating the legal side of being an LGBTQ+ parent is complicated, but it's also filled with love and determination. Each legal document signed and hurdle overcome is a step toward securing your rights and a future where your family can thrive without bounds. As you move forward, remember that securing legal parental status is not just about protecting your family in the eyes of the law; it's about laying down the foundational stones of security, recognition, and permanence that every child deserves.

Evaluating the Financial Costs of Adoption, Surrogacy, and ART

Let's talk numbers—but not the boring kind. Imagine planning a dream vacation, mapping out the sights you'll see and the foods you'll savor, and then realizing you need a budget to make it all happen. Similarly, planning your path to parenthood involves understanding the financial terrain, from the high peaks of surrogacy costs to the more manageable trails of adoption fees, depending on various factors.

First up is adoption. The costs here can vary as wildly as the plot twists in a telenovela. Whether you go through a private agency or opt for a public foster care adoption, expenses can range from little to nothing (in the case of foster care adoptions, which often come with subsidies) to upwards of $40,000 for private domestic and international adoptions. These costs typically cover home study, legal, and agency fees, but remember the travel costs that might pop up if you're adopting from another state or country.

Next up is surrogacy, which can get pretty expensive. Generally, the total can run between $90,000 and $130,000. This budget blockbuster covers everything from the medical expenses of IVF, medications, and prenatal care to compensating the surrogate and covering legal fees to ensure all parental rights are secured. It's a hefty price tag, reflecting the extensive medical and legal work required to ensure a smooth and secure process.

Then there's Assisted Reproductive Technology (ART), including IVF and IUI. Costs here can range dramatically based on how many cycles you go through and whether you need additional services like egg or sperm donation. A single IVF cycle can cost between $12,000 and $17,000, and that's before adding the cost of medications, which can pile on an additional $1,500 to $3,000. IUI is generally less expensive, averaging around $300 to $1,000 per attempt, but remember, it often takes several tries before hitting the jackpot.

Diving into the nitty-gritty of financial planning might not be as exhilarating as planning a Pride parade, but it's equally important. Think of it as crafting a detailed script for allocating your resources. Start with a clear overview of your current financial landscape. How much can you realistically spend without turning your daily life into a financial high-wire act? Consider regular savings plans, perhaps setting aside a fixed percentage of your income towards your family-building fund. Look into health insurance coverage as well—some plans might cover portions of ART procedures or adoption expenses.

Real-life budgeting stories? Sure thing. Take Clara and Morgan, for instance, who opted for IVF. They juggled their finances like circus performers, combining savings with a grant they received from a fertility advocacy group. They also chose a clinic that offered a refund program, providing a safety net that some of the costs could be recouped if the treatments didn't result in a pregnancy. It was a mix of strategic planning and resourceful thinking that helped them manage the financial weight of IVF.

For those feeling the pinch, consider fundraising or exploring grant opportunities. Crowdfunding platforms can rally community support around your parenting dream, turning your network into a tangible pillar of support. Furthermore, numerous grants are available specifically for helping LGBTQ+ individuals and couples with adoption or fertility treatments. Organizations like the Family Equality Council occasionally offer financial assistance programs to ease the burden on prospective parents.

Navigating the financial aspects of family building is undoubtedly complex and can be as daunting as deciding who will be the fun parent. But with careful planning, a clear understanding of the costs involved, and a willingness to explore all available financial support systems, you can plot a financial pathway that leads to your ultimate destination—a family of your own.

Your Support Network Early On

Imagine you're assembling a dream team for the ultimate group project: raising a child. In this scenario, each member—from close friends to professional counselors—plays a pivotal role, offering different forms of support that weave together a safety net, both robust and resilient. The importance of having a support network in LGBTQ+ parenting cannot be overstated; it's like having a toolbox equipped for every imaginable scenario, whether it involves a shoulder to cry on, expert legal advice, or just someone who can run to the store at midnight when you're out of diapers.

Building this network might initially feel daunting—like trying to make friends on the first day at a new school. Start with local LGBTQ+ groups, which can be invaluable. These groups offer a space to meet people who understand your experiences intimately. They often organize events, workshops, and meet-ups that serve as social gatherings and provide educational resources tailored to the needs of LGBTQ+ families. A quick online search or visiting community centers can point you in the right direction. Then, there's the digital world—forums, social media groups, and parenting blogs that offer a platform to connect and provide a wealth of information and shared experiences at your fingertips, accessible from the comfort of your couch.

Next, consider the role of your existing network—friends and family. This circle can offer emotional and sometimes financial support and practical help. It's about quality over quantity; focus on cultivating deeper connections with a few people who truly understand and support your parenting goals and values. Talking openly about your needs and expectations can help strengthen these relationships, making them a reliable support system for tough and happy times.

Professional support is equally crucial. This includes finding LGBTQ+-friendly counselors who can navigate the unique psychological landscape of LGBTQ+ parenting, family lawyers who specialize in LGBTQ+ family law to guide you through legal complexities, and fertility specialists who are not only skilled but also sensitive to the needs of queer individuals. Choosing the right professionals may feel like browsing endless online reviews to find the perfect vacation rental, hoping it lives up to the pictures. Start with recommendations from within your community, and don't hesitate to interview these professionals to ensure they align with your family's needs and values.

The tales of support networks in action are both heartwarming and enlightening. Consider the story of Sam and Finley, a couple who adopted their son, Luca. Throughout their adoption process, they leaned heavily on a network of other adoptive parents who had navigated similar paths. This network was instrumental in guiding them through the paperwork maze and the emotional rollercoaster of adoption. They also joined a weekly group therapy session with other LGBTQ+ parents, providing a space to share their experiences and feelings in a supportive environment. Then there's Reese, a trans dad who found invaluable support through a local LGBTQ+ parenting group, which connected him with a counselor specializing in gender identity, helping him navigate his transition in the context of fatherhood.

Building and maintaining a support network is an ongoing process that evolves as your family's needs change over time. It requires effort, openness, and sometimes the courage to seek help. But the rewards—a community that holds you up, gives you strength and celebrates your family—are immeasurable. As you forge these connections, remember that every phone call to a friend, every professional consultation, and every group meet-up weaves another strand into the safety net that supports your family's journey.

First Steps to Parenthood: Checklists for LGBTQ+ Prospective Parents

Embarking on the path to parenthood is like preparing for a grand adventure that requires careful planning, a bit of know-how, and a lot of heart. Getting started can feel overwhelming —like standing at the base of a mountain, looking up, wondering just how you'll make it to the peak. But worry not! A well-thought-out checklist can serve as your trail map, guiding you through the initial crucial steps confidently and clearly.

Preparation Checklist

First things first, let's talk health checks. It's not just about catching up on vaccinations or getting a clean bill of health— though those are important, too! This is about comprehensive screenings and consultations to ensure you're in tip-top shape for the demands of parenthood. This includes fertility assessments if you're considering biological options like IVF or IUI. Regular check-ups with your healthcare provider can set a strong foundation, ensuring you're as healthy as possible as you enter this new phase of life.

Next up, legal consultations. It's crucial to understand the legal landscape that will surround your future family. This means consulting with attorneys specializing in family law within the LGBTQ+ community. They can provide invaluable insights into your rights and help you navigate the complexities of adoption laws, surrogacy agreements, and parental rights. Think of it as gathering your gear before a hike; you wouldn't start without the right equipment, so why start your family-building adventure without the necessary legal preparations?

Financial reviews are equally essential. Parenthood, regardless of your route, can be a significant financial undertaking. Reviewing your finances helps set realistic expectations and prepares you for upcoming expenses. This includes setting up a savings plan for immediate and future costs, reviewing your insurance to understand what aspects of family-building it covers, and perhaps considering a consultation with a financial advisor who can help map out a budget that includes potential costs like adoption fees or medical treatments for surrogacy or ART.

Decision-Making Tools

Choosing between adoption, surrogacy, or biological parenting methods can feel like standing at a crossroads without a signpost. To aid in this decision, consider tools like decision matrices or pros-and-cons lists tailored to LGBTQ+ family-building. These tools help you weigh factors such as the desire for a biological connection versus the potential speed of adoption processes, the financial implications of each method, and the emotional journey you're prepared to undertake. Each family's criteria will differ, so personalized tools that reflect your specific circumstances and values can guide you toward the right decision.

Initial Steps for Different Paths

For those leaning towards adoption, the initial steps involve researching accredited agencies that are LGBTQ+ friendly and understanding the types of adoption available—be it open, closed, domestic, or international. To gain a deeper understanding of the process, attend informational meetings often required by agencies.

If surrogacy is your chosen path, start by researching reputable surrogacy agencies that have experience working with LGBTQ+ families. Initial consultations with these agencies can clarify the surrogacy journey, including selecting a surrogate that matches your criteria.

For prospective parents looking at IVF or IUI, the first steps include finding fertility clinics with inclusive practices and strong track records with LGBTQ+ families. Initial consultations with fertility specialists will help determine your options based on medical evaluations and discuss the different protocols, such as using donor sperm or eggs.

Resources and Contacts List

Equip yourself with a robust list of resources and contacts. This should include:

- LGBTQ+ Parenting Groups: Organizations like the Family Equality Council offer support and resources for LGBTQ+ parents and hold events that can provide both community connection and practical advice.

- Legal Advisors: Look for law firms specializing in LGBTQ+ family law. Organizations such as Lambda Legal can offer referrals.
- Fertility Clinics: Clinics like the Pacific Fertility Center in Los Angeles, which are known for their work with LGBTQ+ individuals and couples, can provide the specialized care needed for family-building options like IVF and IUI.
- Financial Advisors: Especially those experienced in planning for family-building costs can provide guidance tailored to your financial situation.

You lay a solid groundwork for your family-building adventure by methodically addressing each area. It's about moving forward with intention and support, ensuring you're as prepared as possible when you decide to take those initial steps toward parenthood. With your health checked, legal ducks in a row, finances reviewed, and a clear decision-making framework, you're not just dreaming of becoming a parent—you're actively building the path there.

TWO

Conception and Family Building

W elcome to the exciting world of conception and family building! Imagine yourself as an artist about to paint your masterpiece. But instead of brushes and paints, your tools are the various methods of conception available to you. It's a deeply personal and transformative phase of life, filled with decisions that shape not just the canvas of your family but the very art of your life. In this chapter, we'll focus specifically on In Vitro Fertilization (IVF), a remarkable option that has enabled countless LGBTQ+ couples to fulfill their dreams of parenthood.

Exploring IVF: Considerations for LGBTQ+ Couples

Understanding the IVF Process

IVF can seem as complex as launching a moon mission, but fear not! Let's break it down into manageable stages. First up, the process begins with the suppression of natural hormonal cycles, followed by hormone therapy to boost egg production. Think of it as revving up your engine before a big race. Once the eggs are ready, they're retrieved in a procedure that's usually quick, though it might require a day or two for recovery—the perfect time for binge-watching or catching up on a good book!

Next, the magic of science takes center stage. The retrieved eggs meet sperm in a lab—this can be donor sperm or sperm from another parent in the relationship, depending on your family plan. Fertilization happens, and voila! Embryos begin to form. These little bundles of cells grow for a few days before one or two are selected for transfer. The chosen embryo is then introduced into the uterus, and then it's a waiting game—a two-week wait that might feel longer than a season finale cliffhanger.

For LGBTQ+ couples, IVF often involves donor sperm or eggs. Selecting a donor can feel like online dating, sifting through profiles to find the right match. It's important to consider everything from medical history to personal interests, as this person will be a biological parent to your child.

Legal Considerations

Now, let's navigate the legal framework. When donors are involved, things can get as intricate as a season of legal dramas. Establishing custody rights over embryos and ensuring legal parenthood for both partners is crucial. Legal agreements with donors should clearly state that the donor relinquishes all parental rights. This is crucial to prevent any legal challenges down the road.

Additionally, for LGBTQ+ couples, especially where one partner is biologically related to the child and the other is not, it's advisable to complete a second-parent adoption. This process secures the non-biological parent's legal rights, ensuring both of you are recognized as legal parents. It's like double-locking your doors—an extra step for security.

Choosing the Right Clinic

Selecting an IVF clinic is like picking a school for your child; you want the best fit. Look for clinics with experience in working with LGBTQ+ families, as they are more likely to understand your specific needs and offer a supportive environment. Questions to ask might include their success rates with donor eggs or sperm, their familiarity with the legal aspects of LGBTQ+ family building, and any support services they offer for LGBTQ+ patients. It's not just about the stats but also about feeling respected and understood.

Personal Stories and Outcomes

Now, for a dose of reality through the stories of those who've walked this path. Take Mark and Carlos, who went through IVF using a gestational carrier. They faced challenges ranging from selecting an egg donor to dealing with multiple failed embryo transfers. But their story is one of ultimate success— twins! Then there's Jenna and Leah, who experienced the emotional rollercoaster of IVF, from the joy of a positive pregnancy test to the heartache of miscarriage, before finally welcoming their daughter. These stories are not just tales of medical procedures; they are journeys of hope, resilience, and the incredible lengths we go to for the love of family.

As you consider IVF, remember it's more than just a series of medical steps. It's a journey toward creating life shaped by love, legal considerations, and the science of possibility. Whether browsing donor profiles or selecting the right clinic, each step you take is a brushstroke in the masterpiece of your family story.

Understanding IUI and AI

Let's dive into the world of Intrauterine Insemination (IUI) and Artificial Insemination (AI), two popular and less invasive methods that might just be your ticket to starting or growing your family. Picture IUI as a VIP pass for sperm—direct access right to the main event, the uterus, aiming for a quicker and more efficient route to fertilization. It's particularly useful when there are issues with sperm mobility or when using donor sperm. AI, often referred to as intracervical insemination, is its less technical sibling, where sperm is placed near, but not directly inside, the cervix. Think of it as a drop-off at the entrance rather than a direct escort inside.

Why choose one over the other? IUI is generally more effective due to the direct placement of sperm in the uterus, increasing the chances of conception. It's the go-to if you're using frozen sperm or if there are known issues that might impede sperm's motility. Conversely, AI is less invasive and more comfortable if looking for a procedure closer to natural conception. It's often preferred by couples who want to try it at home, adding personal intimacy.

Choosing a sperm donor is a chapter in your family-building story that requires careful consideration. It's about more than just picking a donor; it's about understanding the implications of known versus anonymous donors. Known donors, perhaps friends or acquaintances, can offer a personal connection and a clear medical history. There's comfort in knowing the biological background of the person helping you in your quest to become a parent. However, this option has complex emotional dynamics and potential legal implications. It's crucial to have clear agreements to define boundaries and parental rights, ensuring no future disputes over custody or visitation.

Anonymous donors, typically chosen through a sperm bank, offer a different kind of comfort: privacy and less emotional complexity. These donors undergo thorough health screenings, and their histories are documented extensively, providing peace of mind regarding health and genetic issues. Yet, this option may leave some unanswered questions about the donor, which could become points of curiosity for the child in the future. Whichever route you choose, consider the emotional and legal long-term implications. Don't hesitate to seek guidance from legal advisors to ensure that all parental rights are established and protected.

Understanding the costs associated with IUI and AI is crucial as you plan your path to parenthood. Consider this as budgeting for a significant project, where every detail must be accounted for to avoid surprises. IUI typically costs between $300 to $1,000 per cycle, not including the cost of donor sperm or any necessary hormonal treatments, which can add several hundred dollars to each cycle. AI is often less expensive, particularly if performed at home, but still involves costs for donor sperm and any legal fees associated with donor agreements. While some insurance policies cover these procedures, coverage varies widely, so it's wise to delve into the specifics of your policy to understand what's covered and what's out-of-pocket.

Embarking on IUI or AI can be an emotional rollercoaster. It's a journey filled with highs as you take proactive steps towards having a child and potential lows as you face the possibilities of unsuccessful attempts. Managing expectations is key. Hope for the best, but prepare for the possibility that it might take several cycles to achieve a successful pregnancy. Many couples find it helpful to connect with support groups or counselors who specialize in fertility issues, providing a space to express emotions and receive support from others who understand the ups and downs of this path.

Remember, whether you're navigating the technicalities of IUI, pondering the personal implications of choosing a known or anonymous donor, budgeting for multiple cycles, or handling the emotional aspects of this journey, you're not alone. Many have walked this path before you, armed with hope and a deep desire for parenthood, and have found success and fulfillment on the other side. As you consider these options, take the time to gather information, seek support, and make the choices that best suit your family's needs and dreams.

Ethical Surrogacy: Finding the Right Match and Legal Protection

Embarking on the surrogacy journey is like setting sail into a vast ocean of possibilities, where the hopes of creating a family meet the complexities of human relationships and legal frameworks. To navigate these waters smoothly, it's essential to have a solid surrogacy agreement in place. Think of it as your navigational chart, guiding you safely through potential storms and ensuring that all parties involved—the intended parents, the surrogate, and, yes, the future child—are protected.

A comprehensive surrogacy agreement covers every conceivable detail, from medical and psychological screenings to financial arrangements and, most critically, the legal rights of all involved. It should clearly outline each party's responsibilities and expectations, including how medical expenses will be handled, compensation for the surrogate, and procedures for handling any potential complications. But it's not just about logistics and finances; it's about ensuring respect and understanding throughout this deeply personal process. The agreement should also detail the process for establishing parental rights once the child is born, typically involving a pre-birth order that legally recognizes the intended parents as the legal parents, bypassing the need for adoption after birth.

Finding the right surrogate is another chapter in your surrogacy story, filled with its own set of hopes and anxieties. It's about more than finding someone who meets the medical criteria; it's about finding a connection and a shared understanding of the significance of this journey. Agencies that specialize in surrogacy can play the role of matchmaker. They help ensure that surrogates and intended parents share similar values and expectations, facilitating meetings and discussions that can help you assess whether there's mutual trust and respect. Consider asking potential surrogates about their motivations, their support system, and their expectations about the relationship during and after the pregnancy. Remember, this relationship is as personal as it gets, and choosing someone with whom you can build a bond based on mutual respect and empathy is crucial.

Navigating the legal protections involves more than just drafting a surrogacy agreement. It includes ensuring the agreement complies with state laws, which vary widely. In some places, surrogacy agreements are fully enforceable, while in others, they may not be recognized. This is where having a skilled attorney becomes invaluable. They can help you understand the legal landscape of your state and ensure that your agreement protects your rights and anticipates any legal challenges that might arise. They'll also help you manage the legal process of establishing your parental rights through pre-birth orders or other necessary legal steps, ensuring that you are legally recognized as their parent from the moment your child arrives.

Ethical considerations in surrogacy are paramount. The surrogate's rights and the importance of informed consent are at the heart of these considerations. It's crucial that surrogates fully understand the medical procedures they will undergo, the physical and emotional demands of pregnancy, and the legal implications of their agreement with the intended parents. Informed consent isn't just a legal formality; it's a continuous process that ensures the surrogate makes informed decisions throughout the pregnancy. Also, surrogates should have independent legal counsel to protect their interests. This counsel should confirm that the surrogate has the freedom to make decisions about her health and pregnancy, including the right to medical care of her choosing and the right to terminate the pregnancy if necessary, according to the terms of the agreement.

The ethical aspects of surrogacy also involve considerations of compensation. While compensation for surrogates is common and can help make the dream of parenthood a reality for many, it's important to approach this aspect with sensitivity and care. Compensation should be fair and clearly outlined in the surrogacy agreement, compensating the surrogate for the physical and emotional investment of carrying a pregnancy without crossing the line into ethical concerns about coercion or exploitation.

Navigating surrogacy includes dealing with complex relationships, legal issues, and ethical questions. Yet, at its core, it remains a journey of hope and love—a path to bringing a new life into the world that can be fulfilling and joyous for everyone involved when navigated thoughtfully and ethically. Whether drafting the surrogacy agreement, choosing the right surrogate, or navigating the legal protections, remember that each step on this path is part of building the family you've dreamed of, underpinned by respect, understanding, and ethical integrity.

Adoption for LGBTQ+ Families: Agencies, Processes, and Expectations

When it feels like your family puzzle is missing a piece, adoption can be the beautiful process that finds that missing piece, lovingly placing it where it belongs. But before diving into the sea of paperwork and interviews, the first step is choosing the right adoption agency. Imagine you're picking a guide for a trek in an unknown land—the agency's role is to navigate you through the complex terrain of adoption. Opt for LGBTQ+ friendly agencies, which show an understanding of your unique family dynamics and provide a supportive, non-judgmental environment. Key indicators of a good agency include explicit non-discrimination policies, experience with LGBTQ+ families, and staff training on LGBTQ+ issues. Watch out for red flags like lack of fee transparency or hesitance to provide references from previous LGBTQ+ clients. Remember, this agency will be your companion on this journey; you want someone who understands and respects your family.

The adoption process itself is like a marathon, not a sprint. It begins with an application that feels more like a tell-all autobiography than paperwork. Following this, the home study assesses your readiness to parent—a series of interviews and home visits to evaluate your living environment and parenting philosophies. Don't sweat the home visits too much; no one expects a show home. They're looking for a safe, loving environment where a child can thrive. Next up is the matching phase, where agencies work to find a child whose needs your family can meet. This phase can be emotionally charged, filled with anticipation and anxiety. It culminates in the finalization of the adoption, a legally binding procedure that officially makes you a parent. It's the day you've been waiting for, where nerves and excitement collide as your family officially grows.

The challenges during this process can sometimes feel insurmountable. LGBTQ+ individuals might face biases or misconceptions from agency staff or the biological parents of the child. Preparation is key. Equip yourself with knowledge about your rights, and don't hesitate to advocate for yourself. Building a support network with other LGBTQ+ adoptive parents can provide not only emotional backing but also practical advice. Remember, every challenge is a step closer to your goal, and resilience is your greatest ally.

Let's talk real-life stories to paint a clearer picture of this journey. Consider Bailey and Jordan, a gay couple who faced a winding road to adopting their daughter. They dealt with agencies that weren't as inclusive as advertised and navigated the emotional whirlwind of being paired with and then rejected by several prospective birth mothers. Yet, their persistence paid off, leading to the adoption of their daughter, Mia, in a moment that was nothing short of magical for them. Then there's

Sophia, a single transgender woman who adopted her son, Eli. She faced hesitation from agencies unsure about trans parents, but ultimately, her determination led to a successful match. Sophia's story isn't just about the challenges but also about breaking barriers and laying a path for future trans parents in the adoption process.

These stories aren't just tales; they're sources of hope and lessons in perseverance. They show that while adoption can be tough, especially for LGBTQ+ people, it's also incredibly rewarding. As you consider adoption, let these stories inspire you, the challenges motivate you, and the joy of parenting drive you. Each step, each document, and each interview brings you closer to the heartwarming chaos of bedtime stories, skinned knees, and unconditional love that is parenting.

Fertility Preservation for Transgender and Non-Binary Individuals

For many transgender and non-binary individuals, the road to affirming their gender identity intersects with decisions about their future fertility. Fertility preservation can be complex and emotional, involving medical procedures, personal goals, and the tough decisions that will impact the rest of your life. Let's unpack the options available, such as sperm banking, egg freezing, and embryo freezing, explicitly tailored to the needs of transgender and non-binary individuals.

Imagine you're considering a significant life change that aligns your body with your identity, but you also dream of one day being a parent. Fertility preservation offers a bridge between these two profound elements of your life. Sperm banking is an option where sperm is collected and frozen for future use, ideal for those who might start hormone therapy or undergo surgeries that could affect fertility. Egg freezing follows a similar principle; eggs are harvested and stored for future use. For those who have a partner and are certain about their future family plans, embryo freezing—fertilizing an egg with sperm and then freezing the embryos—might be the preferred route. Each of these options provides a way to hold onto the possibility of biological parenthood, even as you pursue a transition that feels right for your gender identity.

Timing and considerations for fertility preservation are crucial and should be carefully considered. The optimal time is typically before beginning hormone therapy, as hormones can affect fertility levels significantly. However, the decision when to preserve fertility is deeply personal and can depend on multiple factors, including your age, relationship status, financial situation, and readiness to start a family. The emotional and psychological readiness to make decisions about future children is also a significant factor, and consulting with a counselor or therapist might provide clarity and support as you navigate these choices.

Access to care can be one of the biggest hurdles. Despite growing awareness, the availability of trans-friendly healthcare providers who can offer fertility preservation services without bias or miscommunication remains a challenge. Finding clinics that provide these services and understand and respect your identity can make a substantial difference in your experience. Resources like the World Professional Association for Transgender Health can offer directories of trans-friendly providers. It's also worth reaching out to local LGBTQ+ community groups who may have recommendations based on firsthand experiences.

Personal narratives from those who have navigated the path of fertility preservation can be incredibly enlightening. Take Jamie, a trans man who chose to freeze his eggs before starting testosterone. He speaks about the dual feelings of excitement for his transition and the poignant sadness at pausing it to undergo fertility preservation. Yet, knowing he has preserved his ability to have biological children provides him with a profound sense of peace. Or consider Skyler, a non-binary individual who used sperm banking, sharing how the decision brought up unexpected feelings about masculinity, fertility, and future parenting roles. These stories underscore the diverse emotional landscapes navigated during this process, highlighting the unique challenges and triumphs faced by transgender and non-binary individuals considering fertility preservation.

As you contemplate fertility preservation, remember it's not just about preserving cells but preserving future possibilities—the dream of one day hearing a little voice call you 'parent.' The journey is deeply personal, sometimes complicated, and filled with hope and the promise of future choices.

Co-parenting Agreements: Legal Advice and Practical

Creating a family as an LGBTQ+ individual or couple often involves unique pathways that might include co-parenting arrangements. Whether it's with a platonic friend, a former partner, or within a polyamorous family, setting up a solid co-parenting agreement is much like putting together a game plan for a team sport. It outlines strategies, anticipates future plays, and sets rules that help everyone involved work toward raising a happy, healthy child.

The importance of a well-crafted co-parenting agreement cannot be overstated. It's your parenting playbook covering everything from day-to-day responsibilities to major decisions. It helps prevent misunderstandings and conflicts by clearly defining roles and expectations. Think of it as a framework that supports building a child's life. Without this structure, life's unpredictability can make parenting more complicated than it needs to be, especially when the parents may not be romantically involved or living together.

Key components of a co-parenting agreement should include decision-making processes, financial responsibilities, and arrangements for custody and visitation. Decision-making processes are crucial because they determine how important decisions are made regarding the child's health, education, and general welfare. Will decisions be made jointly, or will one parent have the final say on certain issues? As for financial responsibilities, the agreement should detail who is responsible for everyday expenses, health care, education, and other costs associated with raising a child. Custody and visitation schedules outline when the child will be with each parent, considering work schedules, holidays, and other factors that affect availability and suitability.

Navigating changes in co-parenting arrangements is another critical aspect covered in the agreement. Life is full of changes —people move, form new relationships, and encounter new challenges. A good co-parenting agreement includes provisions for amending the agreement as circumstances change, ensuring that the child's best interests are always prioritized. This might involve periodic reviews of the agreement or predefined procedures for introducing and negotiating changes.

To give you a real sense of how co-parenting agreements function in diverse families, consider the case of Charlie and Sage, a transgender man and a cisgender woman who decided to co-parent together. They set up a co-parenting agreement detailing everything from how they would handle the costs of extracurricular activities to what would happen if one needed to relocate for work. Their proactive planning helped them navigate Sage's job transfer, which involved moving to a different state. Because they had a plan, they could adjust their co-parenting arrangements smoothly, ensuring their son maintained a strong relationship with both parents.

Another scenario involves Avery and Rowan, a lesbian couple who co-parented with Avery's brother and his husband. Their co-parenting agreement covered the basics of financial and decision-making responsibilities. It included clauses about how the child would be raised in a culturally inclusive environment that honored all four parents' heritages. This foresight proved invaluable in maintaining harmony and shared values across both households.

These case studies highlight how co-parenting agreements can effectively manage the complexities of shared parenting responsibilities, providing a stable and structured environment for children. As you consider setting up your co-parenting agreement, remember that the key is clear communication, mutual respect, and flexibility. With these elements, you can create a supportive and loving framework that allows your child to thrive, no matter how unconventional your family structure.

Figuring out co-parenting agreements shows the complex relationships and responsibilities that make up modern families, especially in the LGBTQ+ community. It underlines the necessity of legal clarity and mutual understanding in crafting arrangements supporting children's and parents' well-being.

As we close this chapter on the various paths to parenthood and the foundational agreements supporting them, we explore the daily realities and joys of raising children within beautifully diverse family structures. The journey ahead is filled with practical insights into navigating day-to-day challenges, celebrating milestones, and fostering your family's growth with love, creativity, and resilience.

THREE

Early Parenthood Challenges and Joys

Welcome to the rollercoaster ride of early parenthood, where every day feels like discovering a new continent—thrilling, a tad overwhelming, and filled with unknowns. For LGBTQ+ parents, this journey often includes a few extra loops on the rollercoaster, especially when securing and protecting parental rights from day one. This chapter is your guide through the maze of legalities and practicalities that form the secure foundation of your growing family.

Ensuring Parental Rights From Day One

Understanding Birth Certificate Protocols

Imagine the birth certificate as the first page of your child's life story—where their legal identity begins. For LGBTQ+ families, ensuring this document accurately reflects parental rights is more than a bureaucratic necessity; it's a crucial step in safeguarding your family's future. The birth certificate that lists both parents, regardless of biological connection, affirms each parent's right to make decisions on behalf of their child and is vital in situations requiring proof of parenthood, such as medical emergencies or enrollment in school.

However, for non-biological parents in LGBTQ+ families, securing a spot on the birth certificate isn't always straightforward. It depends a lot on where you live. In many places, the non-biological parent must complete an adoption process—often referred to as a second-parent adoption—to be listed on the birth certificate. This process solidifies the legal bond between parent and child and closes any gaps that might be exploited by legal challenges in the future.

Navigating State Variability

Every state in the U.S. has its own rules about who can be listed as a parent on a birth certificate, and these rules can be complicated for LGBTQ+ parents. Some states are quite progressive, offering straightforward paths to including non-biological parents on the birth certificate right from birth. Others may require a court order or have other complex requirements requiring a law degree.

To manage this variability, start by getting to know the laws in your state. Consulting with a lawyer specializing in LGBTQ+ family law can be invaluable here. They can provide guidance tailored to your specific situation, helping to ensure that when your little one arrives, all the paperwork is in place to affirm your family's legal structure.

For example, if you live in a state that requires a second-parent adoption, you'll need to start this process well before your child's birth to ensure it's completed as soon after birth as possible. This often involves home visits, background checks, and court appearances—no small feat when preparing to welcome a new child into your home.

Legal Safeguards

Setting up legal safeguards is like installing the most reliable security system for your family. Apart from birth certificate adjustments and second-parent adoptions, ensure you have all necessary legal documentation. This includes medical powers of attorney, which allow you to make health decisions for your child if they are sick or injured. Wills are also crucial, as well as specifying guardianship preferences should something happen to you. It's about preparing for all scenarios to ensure your child is always protected and cared for, no matter what life throws your way.

Advocating for Rights

Advocating for your and your child's rights can sometimes feel like trying to move mountains. Start by thoroughly understanding your rights, then arm yourself with the courage to insist they are respected. If you encounter resistance from hospital staff, schools, or government offices, know who to contact. Organizations like Lambda Legal and the ACLU can be powerful allies in challenging discriminatory practices and securing your family's rights.

For instance, if you find that the hospital where your child was born is reluctant to list both parents on the birth certificate, a letter from a lawyer can often clarify the legal precedents and statutes, encouraging compliance. In more stubborn cases, legal action may be necessary to assert your rights. It's about standing firm, armed with knowledge and expert support, to ensure your family is recognized and protected.

Navigating these early legal waters as an LGBTQ+ parent isn't just about filling out forms and ticking boxes. It's about laying the legal groundwork to support and protect your family through all the joys and challenges. By ensuring these protections are in place from day one, you not only secure your parental rights but also affirm the validity and recognition of your family in the eyes of the law and society.

Navigating Healthcare: Finding LGBTQ+ Friendly Pediatric Care

When preparing to bring a new child into your family, choosing the right healthcare provider is one of your most crucial decisions. It's like casting a pivotal role in the ongoing movie that is your family's life. This person or team will be with you through everything from the sniffles and scraped knees to vaccinations and developmental milestones. For LGBTQ+ families, finding pediatric care providers who are not only competent but also LGBTQ+ friendly and culturally sensitive can feel like searching for a needle in a haystack—but it's essential.

The reason? Inclusive health practices in pediatric care don't just affect your child's well-being; they significantly influence the health of your entire family dynamic. A pediatrician who respects and understands the unique aspects of LGBTQ+ families can become a trusted ally. They can offer guidance that considers all facets of your family's situation, from the social aspects of having same-sex parents visible at school events to the nuances of explaining family relationships in medical history forms.

When scouting for the right pediatric care provider, tap into your local LGBTQ+ community for recommendations. Often, the best leads come from other families who have walked the path before you and can provide first-hand insights into which local practitioners are true allies. Online forums, local LGBTQ+ organizations, and even social media groups dedicated to LGBTQ+ parenting can also be invaluable resources.

Once you have a few names, it's time to prepare for the initial consultation—think of it an audition where you're the director. You want to ask the right questions to ensure this potential healthcare provider is clinically excellent and fits your family's needs well. Here's a checklist of questions to consider:

- How do you approach discussions about family dynamics with children and other healthcare staff?
- Can you provide examples of how you've supported LGBTQ+ families in the past?
- What is your approach to gender identity and sexual orientation in children and adolescents?
- How do you handle confidentiality in sensitive situations, particularly with LGBTQ+ adolescents?
- Are your office forms and patient materials inclusive of diverse family structures?
- How do you and your staff stay informed about the unique health needs and concerns of the LGBTQ+ community?

This initial conversation can reveal much about whether a provider's practice is genuinely inclusive or if their understanding of LGBTQ+ issues is only superficial. You must feel heard, respected, and valued—not just as a patient but as a family.

Despite our best efforts, encountering discrimination in healthcare settings is a harsh reality for many LGBTQ+ families. If you find yourself in a situation where your family is not treated with the respect and care you deserve, it's crucial to know how to advocate for your rights. Begin by documenting every instance of discriminatory behavior or treatment. This record can be vital if you need to escalate your concerns. Reach out to patient advocacy groups who can offer support and guidance on effectively addressing discrimination. In some cases, this might mean filing a formal complaint with the medical facility or taking legal action, steps that can feel daunting but are sometimes necessary to protect your family and pave the way for better treatment for other LGBTQ+ families.

Remember, the goal is to build a healthcare support system that feels like an extension of your family—one that nurtures and protects, understands and respects, just as any family should. Finding and choosing the right healthcare providers is not just about medical expertise; it's about forming a team that supports all aspects of your family's well-being.

Bonding with Your Baby: Tips for LGBTQ+ Parents

Bonding with your newborn is like tuning into a new and exciting frequency on life's radio, where every little coo, smile, and stretch is a precious signal of a deepening connection. For

LGBTQ+ parents, creating a bond with your baby carries profound joy along with unique dynamics. Let's explore some particularly effective bonding strategies that cater to the distinctiveness of LGBTQ+ family structures.

Skin-to-skin contact, often called kangaroo care, is a wonderful place to start. It's as simple and lovely as it sounds - holding your baby close against your skin. This practice is not only for birthing parents but can be equally magical for non-biological parents, helping to forge essential connections early on. During these serene moments, your heartbeat and warmth comfort your newborn, and hormones that enhance bonding and reduce stress are released in both of you. Imagine those quiet mornings, with the soft light filtering through the window, sharing the warmth and calm with your child; these moments build the foundation of a lifelong bond.

Shared feeding times also offer pivotal bonding opportunities. Whether breastfeeding, bottle-feeding with expressed milk, or using formula, these times are about much more than nutrition. They are moments of closeness, eye contact, and gentle conversation. For non-biological parents, taking turns in feeding involves you actively in caregiving and establishes you as a source of comfort and security. Picture those midnight feeds, where it's just you and your baby awake in the quiet of the night, a time that can feel surprisingly intimate and special.

Responsive caregiving is about tuning into your baby's cues and responding to their needs sensitively and consistently. It's about learning the unique language of your child's cries, gurgles, and silences and responding with comfort and care. This dance of action and reaction is about meeting needs and communicating love and safety to your baby. Each time you soothe their cries, change a diaper, or sing a soft lullaby, you tell them, "I am here for you," reinforcing their trust and attachment.

Navigating your family's unique dynamics is also crucial in the bonding process. As your child grows, explaining different family roles in ways they can understand is important. This might involve simple stories about your family structure or using photo books that include various family types. It's about normalizing your family's composition so that your child sees their family reflected in the stories and images around them.

Regarding resources, some wonderful books and media celebrate diverse family forms and can be part of everyday interactions. For example, *And Tango Makes Three*, a charming tale about a real-life penguin family with two dads, can be a delightful addition to your bedtime story routine. Not only does it mirror the normalcy of various family setups, but it's also a fun way for your child to see reflections of their own family in the wider world.

Community support, too, plays a pivotal role in enhancing these bonding experiences. Engaging with LGBTQ+ parenting groups or online forums can provide spaces to share experiences, gain advice, and feel supported by others who understand the nuances of LGBTQ+ parenting. These communities can be beneficial when you need to feel connected or seek family-friendly activities where diverse family structures are celebrated and welcomed.

Creating a bond with your baby is a journey filled with tender moments and learning experiences. As you navigate this path, remember each family is unique, and so is each bond. Whether through the warmth of skin-to-skin contact, the shared quiet of feeding times, the attentive response to your baby's needs, or the support of your community, you are laying down the stones on the path of a lifelong, loving relationship with your child. Though sometimes challenging, these early days are incredibly precious and form the bedrock of your family's future.

Dealing with Microaggressions and Discrimination as New Parents

Navigating the world as new parents is like learning a new dance. You step forward, sometimes you stumble, and occasionally, you might step on each other's toes. For LGBTQ+ parents, this dance can often be complicated by microaggressions and outright discrimination, subtle yet pervasive reminders that some parts of society still have a ways to go in understanding and accepting diverse family structures. Identifying these microaggressions is the first step in this complex choreography. They can appear innocuous, like the constant questioning of "Who's the real parent?" or the presumptuous "What did your kids do for Mother's/Father's Day?" These questions might not seem malicious, but they chip away at your sense of legitimacy and can be emotionally draining.

The cumulative impact of these microaggressions on your mental health can be profound. Over time, they can lead to increased stress, anxiety, and even depression, clouding the joyous experience of new parenthood. Recognizing them for what they are—validating societal biases rather than reflecting on your parenting—is crucial. This awareness empowers you to address them internally and in your interactions with others, turning each encounter into an opportunity for subtle education and advocacy.

When it comes to responding to microaggressions and discrimination, having a strategy is key. It's about choosing your battles and deciding when to engage, educate, or simply walk away, all while protecting your peace. In personal settings, such as family gatherings or among friends, clarifying misconceptions with gentle corrections can foster understanding and change. For instance, explaining each parent's roles in your child's life can help reshape outdated perceptions of family roles. In public scenarios, like dealing with unsolicited comments in the park, a firm yet polite correction might suffice, such as, "We're all real parents here, loving and raising our child together."

Legal protections form an essential shield in your arsenal against discrimination. Familiarize yourself with the laws in your area concerning LGBTQ+ rights, particularly those related to family and parenting. Legislation varies widely, but knowing your rights is the foundation of your defense. In the U.S., for instance, the Civil Rights Act and specific state laws protect against discrimination based on sexual orientation and gender identity. If you face discrimination that escalates beyond casual microaggressions—perhaps from institutions like schools or healthcare providers—knowing the legal steps you can take and the resources available, such as contacting the ACLU or tapping into local LGBTQ+ legal aid services, can provide a clear course of action.

Despite these challenges, I always appreciate the importance of self-care and resilience. These are buzzwords and vital practices that sustain your family's well-being. Create a self-care routine that includes activities that nourish both your body and mind, like regular exercise, hobbies that you enjoy, or simply quiet time to decompress. Foster resilience by building a community with other LGBTQ+ families with similar experiences. This network can be a source of support, advice, and solidarity, helping you to feel less isolated and more empowered. Engaging in advocacy through local groups or national organizations can reinforce your sense of agency and purpose, turning negative experiences into catalysts for change and strengthening your family's resilience.

In dealing with microaggressions and discrimination, remember that you are not just defending your own family's validity; you are also paving the way for future LGBTQ+ families to experience a more accepting world. Each informed response, legal stand, and self-care moment add up, contributing to a broader cultural shift towards inclusivity and respect. As you navigate these challenges, hold onto the joy and love that define your family, letting them guide you through the complexities of early parenthood.

Celebrating Milestones in Unique Ways

When marking the special moments in your family's life, why stick to the script when you can write your own? Creating new traditions for your LGBTQ+ family is more than just fun—it's about reflecting your values, culture, and love in your daily life. Each celebration is a part of your family's story, shaped by the joy of shared experiences.

Encouraging LGBTQ+ parents to innovate traditions means turning the lens on what makes your family special. Maybe it's celebrating the anniversary of the day your child came home— an 'Adoption Day' celebration with as much fanfare as a birthday. Or perhaps it's a 'Gotcha Day' for the day you completed the adoption process, marked by a family outing or a storytelling night where you recount how your child came into your life, ensuring they know their story is cherished. These traditions serve as milestones that not only commemorate important events but also reinforce the bonds of your family and affirm the journey you've embarked on together.

When planning celebrations, consider inclusive ideas and reflect the diversity of family structures. For instance, hosting a non-gendered birthday party can be a delightful way to ensure every child feels included. This could involve themes that are universally loved, like animals or outer space, and activities that aren't tied to gender norms, like treasure hunts or craft stations. Similarly, holiday celebrations can be tailored to reflect your family's unique makeup. If your family structure includes more than two parents, perhaps due to polyamory or a co-parenting arrangement, consider inclusive activities that allow each parent a role, ensuring everyone feels valued and included.

Sharing these personal milestone celebrations within your community network can be incredibly powerful. It allows others to see and celebrate your family's joys and inspires other LGBTQ+ families to navigate similar paths. Consider sharing your experiences at community gatherings, through local LGBTQ+ organizations, or on social platforms dedicated to LGBTQ+ families. These stories can light the way for others and strengthen the network of support that binds the community together.

Documenting your family's milestones is equally important. It's about creating a legacy, a tangible connection to the past for your child and future generations. This could be through photo books that include photos and little notes about what each milestone meant to the family. Or why not start a family blog?

Share stories of your unique celebrations, the highs and lows, and the lessons learned. This acts as a personal journal and a resource for other families. Each post, each photo, and each story adds another patch to your family's quilt, enriching the narrative with the richness of lived experience.

In crafting these new traditions and celebrating each milestone, you're doing more than just throwing a party or snapping photos—you're affirming your family's identity and creating a space where love, in all its forms, is celebrated. These moments are the pillars that will support your child's understanding of their story, giving them a sense of belonging and pride in their unique family history. As you plan and celebrate each of these special moments, remember you're not just passing on traditions; you're passing on a legacy of love and acceptance.

The Role of Chosen Family in Early Parenthood

In LGBTQ+ lives, chosen family bonds are especially strong and important. Chosen family refers to the close bonds we form with people not related to us by blood but chosen through mutual respect, support, and love. For many in the LGBTQ+ community, these bonds are not just additions to our lives; they are essential supports that hold us up, celebrate our joys, and help us navigate the complexities of life, including parenting.

Integrating your chosen family into your parenting journey can transform the experience from managing responsibilities to profoundly enriching your family's life. These are the friends who can babysit when you desperately need a break, the honorary uncles and aunts who bring joy and wisdom into your child's life, or even the chosen siblings who stand by you during challenging times, offering a shoulder to lean on. To make these important relationships a part of your daily life, include them in regular family routines. Invite them to join you for weekend picnics, birthday celebrations, or a casual dinner at home. Over time, these shared experiences can deepen bonds, creating a robust support network that feels as foundational as relatives by blood.

However, the role of the chosen family isn't just about the emotional and practical support they provide. There are legal considerations to consider, particularly regarding your child's welfare. For instance, should anything happen to you, who would care for your child? Setting up legal safeguards like guardianship in your will for trusted chosen family members can ensure your child remains cared for by people who truly understand and respect your family values. Additionally, consider legal permissions for medical decisions—having forms that allow chosen family members to make medical decisions or even just take your child to a doctor's appointment can be crucial in emergencies.

The stories of support the chosen family provides are heartwarming and illuminating. Take, for example, Chris and Dakota, a gay couple with a newborn daughter. Their chosen sister, Jessica, has been a pillar in their parenting journey. Jessica's involvement has been a game-changer, from accompanying them to prenatal appointments to stepping in as a caregiver when they needed to rest. She's not just a helper; she's a part of the family, cherished and relied upon. Or consider Frankie, a single lesbian mother whose chosen brother, Luis, has been her rock. Luis has been there for every milestone, from Frankie's daughter's first steps to her first day of school. His support has helped Frankie manage the practicalities of parenting and brought a masculine presence into her daughter's life, enriching her world.

These stories highlight how chosen family members often step into roles that biological families traditionally fill, bringing unique perspectives and strengths that enhance the parenting experience. They also underscore the importance of recognizing and formalizing the roles of chosen family members to ensure they can continue to provide support in ways that align with legal norms and societal expectations.

As you reflect on the role of your chosen family in your own life, consider the joy and support they bring and the ways you can formally acknowledge and integrate them into your family structure. Whether through legal means or the weaving of daily routines, these chosen bonds can significantly bolster your journey through parenthood, ensuring that no matter what challenges arise, you have a family of choice standing with you, ready to face whatever comes your way.

In wrapping up this chapter on the early challenges and joys of parenthood, we've explored the practicalities of navigating this new terrain and the profound impact of a chosen family. As we move forward, remember that each step in this journey is an opportunity to strengthen the bonds that support and enrich your family life. Looking ahead, the next chapter will delve deeper into the evolving dynamics as your child grows, continuing to offer guidance and support tailored to the unique needs of LGBTQ+ families.

FOUR

Education and Community Integration

Navigating preschool as LGBTQ+ parents can be challenging and confusing. But fear not! This chapter is your trusty compass, guiding you through the intricacies of advocating for inclusivity within preschool settings, ensuring these environments are as welcoming and affirming as a warm hug.

Understanding Preschool Policies

The first step in this journey is understanding the lay of the land—or, in this case, the preschool policies. Like little communities, their diversity and inclusivity policies shape preschools' cultures and norms. It's crucial to start by researching these policies, as they set the tone for your child's environment. Think of it as doing detective work; you're gathering clues on how well your family will be supported and represented.

Start by looking at the school's mission statement and diversity clause, often available on their website or parent handbook. These documents can provide significant insights into the school's commitment to creating an inclusive environment. However, don't stop there. Schedule a visit and chat with the staff. Ask questions like, "Can you share examples of how you've supported LGBTQ+ families?" or "How is diversity celebrated in classroom activities and curriculum?" Their responses can offer a peek into the everyday realities of the school's inclusivity.

Another great approach is to attend a parent-teacher meeting before making your decision. Here, you can observe firsthand how inclusive the conversations are. Are same-sex parents acknowledged when discussing family-related activities? Are there books and materials that include diverse family structures? These details matter because they reflect whether the school not only talks the talk but also walks the walk in supporting all families.

Advocacy Strategies

Armed with your insights on the preschool's policies, you should advocate for more inclusivity. This is your chance to make a difference—not just for your child, but for others who will come to that preschool after you. Effective advocacy often starts with open communication. Meet with school administrators to discuss your family's needs and perspectives. Bring along resources to help the school understand these needs, like articles, books, or guidelines from reputable LGBTQ+ advocacy organizations.

When advocating, remember that it's not just about voicing concerns but also about collaborating to find solutions. For example, if the school lacks books that reflect diverse family structures, perhaps suggest organizing a book drive or donating a few favorites from your collection. These actions address the gaps and position you as a proactive and supportive school community member.

Resource Sharing

Sharing resources is like planting seeds in a garden; it's about nurturing growth and understanding through education. If you've found certain books, toys, or materials particularly effective in explaining and celebrating LGBTQ+ diversity, share these with your child's preschool. Many educators appreciate having tools that can help them explain complex topics in age-appropriate ways.

For instance, books like "The Family Book" by Todd Parr or "And Tango Makes Three" by Justin Richardson and Peter Parnell can be wonderful additions to a classroom. They tell engaging stories that impart understanding and respect for different family dynamics. You could create a small resource pack for the school, including a list of such books, links to helpful educational videos, and guides from LGBTQ+ educational organizations.

Building Alliances

Lastly, building alliances with other parents and educators within the school can amplify your advocacy efforts. Start by connecting with the parent-teacher association (PTA) or similar groups within the school. These platforms can offer opportunities to voice ideas and initiate school-wide inclusivity projects.

Moreover, fostering relationships with other parents can lead to a support network that benefits everyone. When you share your experiences and listen to theirs, you build a community of allies who can advocate for a welcoming and inclusive educational environment. Whether it's organizing an inclusivity workshop for the school or setting up casual parent meetups to share experiences and resources, these alliances can make all the difference in creating a positive change.

By understanding, advocating, sharing resources, and building alliances, you're not just preparing your child for preschool but also helping create an educational environment where every family feels valued and included. As you embark on this process, remember your voice is powerful, your actions impactful, and your role as an advocate not only supports your child but also paves the way for future generations to thrive in more inclusive and understanding community spaces.

Navigating School Policies

Stepping into the world of elementary and secondary education as an LGBTQ+ parent can sometimes feel like navigating a maze blindfolded. You're looking for the best academic environment for your child and a place where your family is respected and protected. Understanding the school's policies on anti-discrimination and bullying is your first line of defense and a crucial step in ensuring your child's well-being. It's about turning the fine print into actionable knowledge. Start by requesting a copy of the school's policies and codes of conduct. You're looking for language that explicitly protects students and families against discrimination based on sexual orientation, gender identity, and family structure. If these protections need clarification, consider this a red flag and a cue for deeper engagement.

The legal protections available to your family can vary significantly depending on where you live. Familiarize yourself with state and federal laws regarding LGBTQ+ rights in educational settings. Tools like the GLSEN State Map from the Gay, Lesbian & Straight Education Network provide a detailed breakdown of existing laws and policies across the United States, helping you understand the legal landscape in your area. Armed with this knowledge, you can effectively advocate for your rights and ensure that the school is not just compliant with the law but also actively supportive of LGBTQ+ students and their families.

Imagine if the school's policies could be better or if you've encountered resistance to inclusivity. This is where your role shifts from observer to advocate. Schedule a meeting with the school administration to discuss your concerns. Bring copies of state or federal guidelines that support your points. It's not just about pointing out flaws but about proposing solutions and offering to help implement them. For instance, if the school lacks a comprehensive anti-bullying policy, you could offer to help develop one by forming a committee that includes teachers, parents, and administrators.

Creating Safety Plans

Consider a safety plan as your child's personal security system, tailored to their needs and ready to activate should they encounter bullying or exclusion. Developing this plan involves collaboration with the school's staff, ensuring they understand the unique risks your child might face and are prepared to act swiftly and effectively. Start by identifying potential risks or issues. Does your child feel vulnerable in certain spaces within the school? Are there particular times of the day when supervision is lax? Discuss these specifics with your child's teacher and perhaps the school counselor to ensure they are aware and proactive in their approach.

The next step is to outline clear steps and responsibilities. Who does your child go to if they feel threatened or upset? What is the process for reporting incidents of bullying? How will the school communicate with you about these incidents, and how quickly? The answers to these questions should be documented in the safety plan. Also, ensure that this plan is accessible—your child and all relevant school personnel should know the plan and understand their roles in it.

For instance, if your child is transgender and uses a different name and pronouns than what's listed on their birth certificate, ensure that teachers are aware and use the correct name and pronouns. This simple act can significantly affect your child's sense of safety and belonging. If a teacher or student fails to respect this, the safety plan should detail how such situations will be corrected and addressed, emphasizing the importance of respect and inclusion.

Inclusion Training for Staff

Inclusion training for school staff and administration is essential for creating a supportive environment for LGBTQ+ students and families. Advocate for ongoing, comprehensive training that covers the nuances of gender and sexual diversity and the specific challenges faced by LGBTQ+ students and families. This training should help educators understand the importance of using correct pronouns, the implications of outing a student, and how to effectively handle bullying or discriminatory behavior.

You might suggest resources or organizations specializing in LGBTQ+ inclusion in schools, such as GLSEN or the Human Rights Campaign, which offer professional development and training programs. Some schools might resist, citing budget constraints or other priorities. Here, you could propose cost-effective solutions like online workshops or partnering with local LGBTQ+ advocacy groups that offer reduced or free training.

Monitoring School Climate

Keeping a pulse on the school's climate is like being a weather forecaster for your child's daily experiences. It involves regular check-ins with your child and their teachers, being attuned to changes in your child's behavior or attitude towards school, and knowing when to act. Encourage your child to share their day-to-day experiences. Create a safe space at home for open conversations about school, friends, and any challenges they might face. This ongoing dialogue can help gauge whether the school's environment is supportive and inclusive.

Additionally, maintain regular communication with school staff. This doesn't just mean attending parent-teacher meetings; it's about actively engaging with your child's education. Volunteer at school events, join the PTA or participate in committees. This visibility can be a powerful tool in ensuring your child's needs are not overlooked and that the school remains accountable for maintaining an inclusive environment.

If you notice signs that the school climate might be becoming less inclusive or safe, don't wait. Bring your concerns to the school's administration immediately. Provide specific examples and ask for concrete steps to address the issue. If necessary, remind them of their legal obligations to provide a safe learning environment for all students, including those from LGBTQ+ families.

By actively engaging with the school system, creating robust safety plans, advocating for comprehensive staff training, and monitoring the school climate, you empower not just your child but pave the way for a more inclusive and supportive educational environment for all LGBTQ+ students. This proactive approach ensures that school becomes a place where every child can thrive and learn in safety and dignity, no matter their background.

Creating Inclusive Spaces in the Community

When you think about community events, imagine them as a mix of different families and individuals, each adding to the diversity. For LGBTQ+ families, being part of these events strengthens your sense of belonging and supports inclusivity. Organizing or influencing these events to be inclusive might seem challenging, but it's like hosting a big family gathering where everyone feels valued and welcomed.

Firstly, diving into community event planning involves collaboration with event organizers. This can be as straightforward as joining the planning committee of your local neighborhood events or school functions. When you're part of the planning process, you have a direct hand in shaping the activities, ensuring they include and celebrate diverse family structures. For example, when planning a community fair or festival, suggest a booth or activity specifically highlighting LGBTQ+ families or culture. It could be a storytelling booth with books that reflect diverse family dynamics or a craft area where kids can create art about their families.

Moreover, the power of visibility and representation should be considered. LGBTQ+ families must be included and visibly celebrated at these events. This could mean featuring LGBTQ+ speakers, performers, or educators who can share their experiences and contributions. Visibility comes in various forms —perhaps a parade float during a community festival celebrating Pride month or a presentation by LGBTQ+ community leaders at a public gathering. These acts of visible inclusion send powerful messages that LGBTQ+ families are a valued part of the community.

Handling resistance is an aspect of community engagement that can't be overlooked. Despite growing acceptance, pushback from certain community members can occur. Here, the key is approaching resistance with firm advocacy and open dialogue. Equip yourself with facts and empathy. For instance, if a community member expresses discomfort about LGBTQ+ inclusive activities at a school event, engage them in a respectful conversation to explore their concerns and share perspectives on the importance of inclusivity for all children's well-being. Sometimes, simply demystifying LGBTQ+ experiences and highlighting common values like love, family, and acceptance can turn resistance into support.

Lastly, celebrating diversity isn't just about including different people; it's about actively embracing and highlighting these differences through themed events and educational activities. Imagine organizing a community picnic where each family brings a dish representing their heritage or culture, paired with stories or mini-presentations. Such events foster a deeper understanding and appreciation of diversity and create a fun, engaging environment where every family can shine and share.

In crafting these events, every decision you make—from the activities you plan to how you handle resistance—builds toward a community that acknowledges and celebrates diversity. This proactive approach ensures that community events are not just gatherings but are vibrant celebrations of our diverse world. Through these efforts, you lay down the stepping stones for a more inclusive community where your family and others like yours can feel truly at home, celebrated, and embraced.

Leveraging Community Resources for LGBTQ+ Families

Navigating parenting as an LGBTQ+ individual or couple can feel overwhelming. Each resource and support system is like a piece of a puzzle that, when put together, creates strong community support and personal empowerment. Finding and using local and online resources for LGBTQ+ families can help you go from just getting by to truly thriving.

Start by scouting out parenting groups and organizations dedicated to LGBTQ+ families. These can be invaluable as they provide support, advice, and a sense of community and belonging. Local LGBTQ+ community centers often host or can connect you to parenting workshops, support groups, or social gatherings. Online websites like COLAGE offer resources and connections for children and families within the LGBTQ+ community. These groups can be beneficial when feeling isolated; they remind you that you're part of a larger community with similar challenges and joys.

Legal aid is another critical resource. Organizations like Lambda Legal or the ACLU have branches or referrals for legal help addressing LGBTQ+ issues. They can guide adoption laws, parental rights, and discrimination, ensuring you have the legal backing to protect and advocate for your family. Engaging with these resources can provide a safety net, reinforcing your confidence to face challenges knowing you have expert support.

Educational workshops are also a treasure trove of information. They can range from teaching legal rights and advocacy skills to offering parenting tips tailored to the needs of LGBTQ+ families. Look for workshops hosted by LGBTQ+ health centers or community groups; they often address topics like navigating the healthcare system, understanding school policies, or even simple everyday parenting tips through an LGBTQ+ lens.

Case Studies: Community Resources in Action

Consider the story of Mica and Sawyer, a lesbian couple who moved to a new city and felt disconnected from supportive networks. They found a local LGBTQ+ parenting group through a community center, which became their lifeline. The group met weekly, providing them with practical parenting advice and deeper connections to families like theirs. Through this group, they learned about a legal workshop that helped them navigate the process of securing Sawyer's legal parentage over their second child, seamlessly integrating crucial legal advice into their family planning.

Then there's the case of Lucas, a trans dad who struggled with isolation in a predominantly conservative area. He connected with an online forum for trans parents, where he found support, understanding, and practical resources shared by others who had walked similar paths. This virtual community became his go-to for advice from gender-affirmative pediatricians to dealing with school administrations, showcasing how online resources can bridge gaps when local support is lacking.

Maximizing Resource Usage

Diving into the available resources can sometimes feel overwhelming, like you're a kid in a candy store but need help figuring out where to start. The key to maximizing these resources lies in active participation and contribution. Engage fully in the groups and workshops you attend; ask questions, share your experiences, and offer insights. Active participation enhances your learning and helps build stronger connections within the community.

Also, consider taking on a leadership or volunteer role within these groups or organizations. This can be a rewarding way to give back and strengthen the resources supporting you. Whether it's organizing an event, leading a workshop, or simply providing peer support, your contribution can enhance the resource's value, not just for you but for all its members.

Resource Networking

Building a network that extends beyond immediate LGBTQ+ circles can enrich your family's support system exponentially. Engage with broader parenting networks, educational organizations, and civic groups. This broadens your support system and fosters greater understanding and inclusivity within the wider community.

For instance, participating in broader parenting workshops or school committees can allow you to bring LGBTQ+ perspectives to more general audiences, promoting inclusivity on a larger scale. It also opens up resources you need access to within smaller community circles, such as specialized parenting programs, educational grants, or broader legal advice.

Using the resources available to LGBTQ+ families, you help your family and strengthen the support networks for the entire LGBTQ+ community. These actions create ripples that enhance the lives of many, building a foundation of understanding, support, and community engagement that lifts everyone involved.

Handling Parent-Teacher Meetings as an LGBTQ+ Parent

Stepping into a parent-teacher meeting can sometimes feel like you're gearing up for a mini-conference where you're both a diplomat and an advocate. It's your stage to discuss, understand, and sometimes enlighten, ensuring your child's needs and experiences as part of an LGBTQ+ family are both understood and respected. Preparation for these meetings isn't just about brushing up on your child's academic performance; it's about setting the scene for a meaningful dialogue about the inclusive support your child needs to thrive.

Let's start with how to prepare for these meetings. It's helpful to think of it as gathering your toolkit. This toolkit should include updates on your child's academic and social progress, any concerns you've observed, and pertinent questions you might have about the curriculum or school policies. But here's where you add another layer—preparing to discuss how being part of an LGBTQ+ family might influence your child's experience at school. For instance, if your child has two moms, ensure the teacher is aware and uses language that reflects this reality, avoiding assumptions about a paternal figure at home. Bring notes or a small document outlining key points about your family structure to help guide the conversation. It's about ensuring the meeting is informative and transformative, fostering an environment where your child feels represented and respected.

Educating educators is another crucial element. While most teachers aim to support all their students, they may not always know the best practices for supporting LGBTQ+ families. Here, you can play a role in gently guiding them. Share resources that have been helpful for you, like articles, books, or links to websites that offer insights into the unique dynamics of LGBTQ+ parenting. For example, sharing a resource like the Human Rights Campaign's "Welcoming Schools" can equip teachers with the tools to handle discussions on family diversity sensitively and effectively. It's about partnering with educators and providing them with the resources to support your child and enhance their professional development in managing diverse classroom dynamics.

Addressing misconceptions is an unavoidable part of these meetings. Despite the best intentions, educators might hold misconceptions about what it means to be part of an LGBTQ+ family. They might wonder about each parent's roles or how to address questions from other students about your child's family structure. Here, clarity and openness come into play. Address these questions head-on, providing clear, calm explanations. It might be something like explaining, "Just like any other family, we all pitch in with homework, bedtime stories, and soccer practice. We just happen to be two dads instead of a mom and a dad." It's about replacing myths with realities, paving the way for a deeper understanding and respect for your family.

Finally, your follow-up strategies after the meeting can make all the difference in ensuring that the agreements and understandings reached during the discussion are implemented. Start by summarizing the key points of your discussion in a follow-up email, thanking the teacher for their time and reiterating any specific steps you've agreed upon. This might include their commitment to using inclusive language or integrating family diversity into classroom discussions. Keep the lines of communication open by checking in periodically to see how things are going and if the agreed-upon measures are being effectively implemented. This ongoing dialogue ensures that the meeting has a lasting impact, reinforcing a supportive and inclusive educational experience for your child.

Navigating parent-teacher meetings as an LGBTQ+ parent involves preparation, education, and advocacy. By entering these meetings well-prepared, ready to educate, and equipped to address misconceptions, you advocate for your child's specific needs and contribute to creating a more inclusive and understanding school environment. Each meeting is an opportunity to strengthen the partnership with your child's educators, ensuring they are aware of and active participants in supporting the rich diversity of all families.

The Impact of Visibility: Participating in Public and Social Media

Stepping into the spotlight as an LGBTQ+ family can feel like being on stage: exhilarating yet exposing. Deciding how visible to be in public and on social media involves balancing your privacy with the powerful pull of advocacy. Think of it as setting the stage for your family's narrative to unfold, where every share, post, or public appearance can shift perceptions and foster understanding. Choosing visibility means weighing the benefits of fostering greater acceptance against the potential risks of exposure to scrutiny or negativity. It's about finding your comfort zone in the spectrum of visibility—from being a vocal advocate to maintaining a more private family life.

When you choose to share your story, whether at community events or on platforms like Instagram or Facebook, you're not just filling feeds with more content; you're challenging norms and broadening the narrative around what family looks like. The power of positive representation cannot be overstated. Seeing LGBTQ+ families enjoying everyday life, celebrating milestones, and navigating challenges provides a counter-narrative to stereotypes and misinformation. It normalizes diverse family structures, making them part of the mainstream tapestry of society. For instance, consider a simple photo of your family picking pumpkins at a local farm. To the casual scroller, it's just another cute family outing. For someone feeling isolated in their LGBTQ+ identity, it's a sign of hope and possibility, showing that happiness and family life are achievable in many ways.

Managing your online presence effectively involves more than just deciding what to post. It's about protecting your family while engaging with a wider audience. Start by familiarizing yourself with the privacy settings on different social platforms. Who can see your posts? Are your photos tagged with locations? Understanding and controlling these settings can help mitigate risks, allowing you to share your life confidently. Additionally, be prepared for negative interactions. Online spaces can be breeding grounds for trolls and unsolicited opinions. Develop a thick skin and a strategy for dealing with negativity—whether it's engaging calmly to educate, using block and report functions, or choosing not to engage. Remember, every online interaction is part of your family's digital footprint; managing this thoughtfully ensures your online world is safe and positive.

The role of LGBTQ+ families as role models can have far-reaching effects. By simply living your truth openly, you inspire others. You show that it's possible to build a loving family as LGBTQ+ individuals, and you pave the way for future generations to do the same with less fear and more support. This visibility is powerful. It impacts those in your immediate community and echoes across society, challenging stereotypes and fostering a culture of inclusivity and acceptance. Consider how sharing your experiences navigating school systems or advocating for inclusive workplace policies can empower others to do the same. Your story becomes part of a larger narrative of progress and change, encouraging others to speak up.

By focusing on visibility, representation, online engagement, and role modeling, your family's story can inspire change and promote understanding. Choosing how and when to share your life helps balance privacy and advocacy, contributing to a world where all families are celebrated for their uniqueness and common humanity. As you engage with your local community and the wider digital world, your family becomes a testament to the diversity and beauty of love in all its forms.

FIVE

Navigating Complexities as Children Grow

As your kids grow up, your journey as an LGBTQ+ parent changes, too. Each stage of your child's growth brings new challenges, especially when explaining your family's structure. This chapter will help you teach your school-aged children about different family dynamics so they can appreciate their family's uniqueness and respect others.

Discussing Different Family Structures with School-Aged Children

Educational Approaches

Imagine you're crafting a mini-curriculum, one that's as engaging as a treasure hunt, where each clue unravels the beauty of diverse family structures. The goal is to make inclusivity a part of everyday learning. Start by integrating simple concepts of diversity into routine conversations. It's like seasoning food —you want it to enhance the flavors, not overwhelm them.

Discuss the different types of families your child might encounter in their storybooks, TV shows, or even in the park. "Look, Josh, that kid has two moms just like you! Isn't that wonderful?" These moments are the building blocks for understanding and respecting family diversity.

Bring this dialogue into playdates and family gatherings, setting the stage for open conversations. Encourage questions and provide answers that celebrate this diversity. If your child asks, "Why does Ellie have two dads?" you can respond with, "Isn't it great how families can be different? What matters is that every family is full of love."

Age-Appropriate Explanations

Your explanations about your family structure need to fit snugly into the understanding of a school-aged child—clear, simple, and straightforward. When discussing donor origins or surrogacy, use analogies that resonate with their world. For instance, explaining a sperm donor could be like explaining how a gardener helps a plant grow by providing seeds. "Just like our garden needed seeds to grow these beautiful flowers, we needed a little help to have you, and that's where our kind donor came in."

When should these concepts be introduced? It's like sensing when a fruit is ripe—timing is crucial. Gauge your child's curiosity and comprehension levels. A question about where babies come from after a family movie can be a natural trigger for these discussions.

School Engagement

Working with your child's school to ensure family diversity is represented can sometimes be challenging, but it is important to ensure everyone feels included and comfortable. Initiate this by meeting with your child's teacher early in the school year to discuss how your family can be represented in school activities and curriculum. Offer to bring books to the class that include diverse family structures or suggest resources that the school might find useful.

For instance, during events like Family Day, ensure that the activities aren't just inclusive but celebratory of family diversity. Propose activities that allow children to share stories about their families through drawings, stories, or show and tell. "My Family" posters can be a fun school project where every child depicts their family members and what they love to do together, highlighting that while families might look different, they all share bonds of love.

Resources for Families

Build your home library with books and materials that reflect diverse family structures. Titles like *Stella Brings the Family* by Miriam B. Schiffer and *The Family Book* by Todd Parr can be wonderful additions. These books mirror the diversity of the real world and open avenues for conversations about inclusivity and respect.

Additionally, recommend these resources to your child's school. Teachers are often looking for materials that help them address diverse topics effectively. By suggesting specific books, programs, or multimedia resources, you can help ensure that the school environment mirrors the inclusivity you teach at home.

Navigating the complexities of raising children in an LGBTQ+ family structure is like mixing colors on a palette. Sometimes, you get unexpected shades, but each adds depth and beauty to the picture. Educating your child about diverse family structures, providing age-appropriate explanations, actively engaging with their school, and enriching your home and educational environment with inclusive resources sets the stage for a world where diversity isn't just accepted—it's celebrated. This chapter aims to arm you with the tools to paint this picture, not just within your home's confines but extending into the broader strokes of society.

Addressing Bullying: Strategies for Parents and Children

Navigating the choppy waters of bullying as an LGBTQ+ parent can sometimes feel like you're trying to calm the storm with a paper umbrella. It's tricky, yes, but not impossible. The key lies in proactivity, empowerment, and a robust support system, ensuring your child knows they're not alone. Let's start by setting up the first line of defense: prevention. Collaborating with your child's school to implement bullying prevention programs that specifically protect children from LGBTQ+ families isn't just about stopping bullies in their tracks—it's about creating an environment where respect and understanding are part of the school's DNA.

Imagine you're planting a garden. You wouldn't just throw seeds on the ground and hope for the best; you'd prepare the soil, making sure it's rich and ready to support growth. Similarly, fostering a school environment that discourages bullying begins with education and awareness. Work with school administrators to integrate diversity training into their programs. Encourage them to include materials and lessons that celebrate different family structures and identities, which can help cultivate a climate of acceptance and respect. This might involve bringing in speakers specializing in diversity, setting up workshops, or updating the school's library to include books that reflect a spectrum of families. Schools that embrace this proactive approach don't just reduce bullying—they enrich their students' perspectives and prepare them to thrive in a diverse world.

Empowering your child to stand up for themselves and others is equally crucial. This doesn't mean teaching them to meet aggression with aggression. Rather, it's about nurturing their self-esteem and their voice. Role-playing can be a powerful tool here. Create scenarios at home where your child can practice what to say or do if someone else is being bullied. Phrases like "Stop, that's not okay!" or "I'm telling a teacher!" are simple yet powerful tools your child can use. These rehearsals can help build their confidence, ensuring that if the time comes, they won't feel frozen or powerless.

Knowing how to respond can make all the difference when bullying occurs. Documenting the incident with as much detail as possible is critical. Teach your child to note who was involved, what was said or done, and when and where it happened. This record is invaluable when communicating with school officials; it turns vague accusations into concrete evidence that can be acted upon. When discussing the incident with school authorities, keep the conversation focused, factual, and forward-looking. It's not just about highlighting a problem but working collaboratively to find a solution. This might involve setting up meetings with the parents of the children involved, discussing changes to supervision during recess, or adjusting how groups are structured in class.

Lastly, don't underestimate the power of a strong support system. Surrounding your child with love and support at home and through external networks can be a tremendous source of comfort and strength. Consider counseling if you feel it might help your child process their experiences. Many therapists specialize in working with LGBTQ+ families and can provide a safe space for your child to express and understand their feelings. Additionally, peer support groups can be invaluable. Connecting with other kids who've faced similar challenges can remind your child that they're not alone, that others have walked this path and come out stronger on the other side.

Navigating bullying requires a multi-faceted approach where prevention, empowerment, direct action, and support play vital roles. By taking proactive steps to work with your child's school, empowering your child to stand up for themselves, effectively handling incidents, and bolstering your child's support network, you create a comprehensive strategy that not only addresses bullying when it happens but also works to prevent it from occurring in the first place. With these strategies in hand, you're better equipped to protect your child and turn their challenges into opportunities for growth and empowerment.

Teenage Years: Navigating Identity and Independence

Supporting your teenager as they explore their own identity, including their sexual orientation and gender identity, can feel a bit like being a gardener nurturing a rare and beautiful orchid. Like each orchid, each teen is unique, requiring specific conditions to thrive. As parents, you provide the environment: the soil, the water, the light. But ultimately, the flower blooms on its own. When it comes to identity exploration, creating an atmosphere of openness and acceptance is key. Start by sharing your own experiences and values around identity, but also make it clear that you're excited to see who they will become on their terms. This encourages your teen to feel safe and supported in exploring and expressing their true self, whatever that may be.

Books, movies, and online resources can be great tools for sparking discussions about identity and diversity. For instance, watching a movie together that features LGBTQ+ characters can open up a conversation about how diverse identities are portrayed in media and what that means in real life. It's also helpful to connect your teen with role models from the LGBTQ+ community, whether through local groups, online platforms, or books and stories highlighting successful and diverse individuals. These connections can provide tangible examples of how diverse identities can be embraced and celebrated, offering your teen more confidence in their journey of self-discovery.

Effective communication is the bridge that connects you to your teenager as they navigate these complex years. It's more than just talking; it's about creating a dialogue. Active listening plays a crucial role here. This means listening to understand, not just to respond. When your teen shares something about their identity or experiences, focus on hearing their feelings and perspectives without rushing to judgment or advice. Phrases like "Tell me more about that." or "How does that make you feel?" can encourage your teen to open up and share more deeply. Regular family check-ins can also be a great way to keep communication channels open. Maybe it's a weekly dinner where everyone shares the highs and lows of their week. These moments can reinforce that you're there for them, no matter what.

Peer pressure is a formidable opponent during the teenage years, and for teens in LGBTQ+ families, it can have additional layers. They might face questions or even criticism about their family structure. Preparing them for these interactions is crucial. Discuss potential scenarios they might encounter and brainstorm how to handle them. Equipping them with factual and respectful responses can boost their confidence. For example, if a peer makes a dismissive comment about their family, they might respond with, "My family might not look like yours, but there's just as much love and support in my home as in any other." Encouraging your teen to surround themselves with supportive friends who respect and embrace diversity can also provide a buffer against negative peer interactions.

As teenagers grow, so does their desire for independence, and it's a big part of their journey towards adulthood. This phase is about balancing freedom with responsibility, from staying out later to navigating social media and online relationships safely. Clear, agreed-upon boundaries and expectations can help manage this transition. Discuss these boundaries openly, explaining their reasons, which can help your teen understand and accept them more readily. For instance, if you're concerned about online safety, discuss the importance of privacy settings and the potential risks of sharing personal information online. Encouraging responsible behavior involves trust and respect on both sides. Show that you trust your teen by giving them responsibilities that foster independence, like managing a monthly budget or making decisions about their extracurricular activities. This boosts their confidence and helps them learn valuable life skills.

Navigating the teenage years as an LGBTQ+ parent means being a guide, a cheerleader, and sometimes a confidant, all rolled into one. It's about supporting your teen's exploration of their identity, maintaining open and honest communication, helping them navigate peer pressure, and guiding them toward responsible independence. These years can be challenging, but with the right approach, they can also be incredibly rewarding, watching your teen grow into their person, ready to take on the world with confidence and self-assurance.

Updating Legal Documentation as Your Child Grows

Managing the ever-evolving landscape of your child's life often means ensuring that all the I's are dotted and T's are crossed on a pile of documents that seem to grow as fast as they do. It's about more than just keeping up; it's about anticipating the changes that come with each new chapter of their lives and preparing accordingly. Staying ahead of the game is crucial regarding legal documentation, particularly in non-traditional family structures. This includes updating names and gender markers on official documents to ensure all legal and healthcare directives are up-to-date.

Let's start with name changes, which might be necessary for various reasons, including gender identity adjustments or simply the desire for a name that better fits. If your child decides to change their name or if it's necessary to update gender markers, navigating the legal processes can feel like decoding a complex puzzle. Each state has its regulations and procedures, which can be daunting. The process typically involves petitioning a court, which might require legal representation and often includes publishing the name change in a local newspaper, although exceptions exist, especially for minors. Engaging with an attorney who specializes in LGBTQ+ family law can provide guidance and ease the burden, ensuring that all forms are correctly filed and legal standards are met. This helps legally affirm your child's identity and empowers them, showing that you fully support their journey to express who they truly are.

As children edge closer to adulthood, updating documents such as guardianship and powers of attorney becomes a pressing task. These documents are essential, especially in emergencies where medical decisions might need to be made. For LGBTQ+ families, it's vital to specify who can make decisions on behalf of your child if you're unable to. Powers of attorney can designate someone you trust to manage healthcare decisions, ensuring your child's welfare is always in trusted hands. Regular reviews of these documents as your child grows, ensure they reflect current wishes and family dynamics, providing peace of mind that your child's care and wishes are clearly articulated and legally recognized in any crisis.

Healthcare rights are another critical area that evolves as your child grows. Understanding how medical consent laws change as your child transitions from minor to young adult is crucial. In most states, the age of medical consent is 18, which means teenagers can start making their own healthcare decisions at this age. For parents, this transition can be nerve-wracking. It is important to discuss these changes with your child and ensure they understand their rights and responsibilities regarding their health decisions. Preparing them might include setting up appointments where they speak with healthcare providers independently, fostering a sense of responsibility and confidence in managing their health. It's also wise to discuss the importance of having a healthcare proxy or durable power of attorney for healthcare, which would allow them to designate someone to make decisions on their behalf should they be unable to do so themselves.

Inheritance and estate planning might not be the first thing on your mind when juggling soccer games and school recitals, but it's crucial to safeguard your child's future. This is particularly important in LGBTQ+ families where legal kinship may not be assumed. Ensuring that your will, trusts, and other estate planning documents reflect your wishes clearly can prevent potential conflicts or legal challenges after you're gone. These documents should detail how you want your assets handled, guardianship directives for younger children, and any specific bequests. Sometimes, setting up a trust can be advantageous, allowing you to specify conditions under which your children can access their inheritance, which can be particularly useful in blended families or unique family situations.

In essence, updating legal documentation as your child grows is about creating a seamless safety net that evolves with them. It's about ensuring that their identity, health, and future are protected and affirmed at every stage of their development, giving you and them the confidence to face whatever life throws your way.

Family Dynamics: Managing Changes as LGBTQ+ Parents

Managing family life can be challenging, especially with big changes like relationship shifts, new siblings, or moving to a new community. Adapting to these new norms requires flexibility, communication, and patience. For instance, if you and your partner are transitioning or introducing your child to a new sibling from a different parent, managing these changes with care and sensitivity is crucial. Start by setting aside time to sit down as a family and openly discuss the changes. If moving to a new area, involve your child as much as possible; let them pick out decorations for their new room or plan a visit to their new school before the move. This inclusion helps them feel like they are part of the process.

Keeping family bonds strong during these changes takes attention and effort. Establishing family rituals can be a wonderful way to ensure these bonds remain strong. This might involve a weekly family game night, a daily dinner together where everyone shares the best and worst parts of their day or a monthly outing to a favorite park. These consistent activities become the bedrock of your family's connection, providing predictable and comforting touchpoints that reinforce the sense of unity and belonging, no matter what changes are swirling around you.

Disagreements are inevitable in any family, more so when navigating the complexities of an LGBTQ+ family structure adapting to changes. Here, effective conflict resolution techniques come into play, ensuring disagreements are a source of growth rather than division. Emphasize the importance of active listening, where each family member feels heard and validated. Teach and practice the art of expressing feelings using "I" statements, such as "I feel upset when..." rather than accusatory "You" statements, which can escalate conflicts. Consider setting up a 'family council' where everyone can air grievances in a structured environment and end each session with a positive resolution or a group hug. This helps resolve issues and models healthy communication strategies for your children.

The complexity multiplies for those navigating the waters of a blended family, where children may have multiple parents and households. Clear communication and defined boundaries are the keys to managing these dynamics effectively. Work with your co-parents to establish consistent rules and expectations across households. This consistency gives children a sense of security and predictability, reducing potential conflicts. Regular meetings with all adults involved ensure everyone is on the same page and can address any issues before they become major problems. Additionally, celebrate the expanded network of care and support that a blended family can offer. Highlight the positives of having a larger family network, such as more people to attend soccer games and school plays and more opportunities for love and support.

Navigating family dynamics as they evolve can be challenging, but with the right strategies and many open hearts, these changes can lead to a richer, more fulfilling family life. By embracing flexibility, fostering open communication, and maintaining a firm foundation of family rituals, you can ensure your family adapts to changes and thrives amidst them.

Supporting Your Child's Exploration of Their Own Identity

Creating a space where your child feels safe and encouraged to explore and express their identity is all about providing the right support and watching them grow. This nurturing space allows them to delve into who they are without fear of judgment, supported by your unconditional love and acceptance. Start by fostering open communication, ensuring that all topics are welcome and nothing is too trivial or profound to be discussed. It's about showing genuine interest and curiosity in their thoughts, feelings, and experiences. This open dialogue creates a foundation of trust and safety that encourages your child to explore their identity more deeply.

Books and media can be powerful tools in supporting your child's identity exploration. They introduce concepts and experiences that may resonate with your child, offering them language and frameworks to understand and articulate their feelings. For younger children, books like *I Am Jazz* by Jessica Herthel and Jazz Jennings can help explain gender identity in a straightforward, accessible way. For older children and teens, *The Gender Quest Workbook* by Rylan Jay Testa provides interactive exercises that explore gender identity. Websites like genderspectrum.org offer extensive resources for parents and children navigating these questions, providing articles, personal stories, and professional guidance.

At some point, professional support may be beneficial, especially if your child is dealing with complex feelings about their identity or encountering challenges related to their LGBTQ+ identity. Psychologists or counselors specializing in LGBTQ+ issues can offer a safe space for your child to explore their identity in depth, supported by expertise in mental health and gender and sexual identity. It's okay to start this conversation by saying, "Sometimes, talking to someone just us can be helpful, especially someone who gets the stuff we're going through." This reassures your child that seeking help is not only okay but also a positive step toward self-discovery.

Celebrating key milestones in your child's identity journey reinforces their self-worth and belonging. This might be celebrating the anniversary of coming out, the acknowledgment of their chosen name, or the first time they express a desire to dress or present in a way that feels true to them. These celebrations can be simple—a special dinner, a thoughtful gift, or a handwritten note that expresses your pride and love. What matters is the recognition and affirmation of their evolving identity, which bolsters their confidence and reinforces the support they have at home.

Navigating your child's journey of self-exploration is a dynamic and ongoing process. It requires patience, openness, and a lot of listening. By creating a supportive home environment, utilizing resources that educate and affirm, seeking professional guidance when needed, and celebrating each step of their journey, you lay down a path of self-love and acceptance for your child. This path strengthens their individuality and deepens the familial bonds that support them through every phase of their life.

The essence of this chapter revolves around nurturing a supportive environment that encourages your child to explore and embrace their identity, whatever it may be. By engaging in open conversations, utilizing resources that educate and affirm, seeking professional support when necessary, and celebrating significant milestones, you help your child navigate their path with confidence and pride. This journey is about discovering who they are and reinforcing the unconditional love and support they have from their family. As we close this chapter and look ahead, we carry forward these themes of love, acceptance, and empowerment into the broader context of maintaining family unity and harmony through all of life's changes.

SIX

Health and Well-Being for LGBTQ+ Families

Picture this: It's another bustling morning at your household. Amidst the whirlwind of breakfast preparations and planning the day, you pause momentarily, taking in the laughter and the occasional bickering that fills the air. It's all part of the dance of family life, isn't it? As LGBTQ+ parents, you navigate a unique rhythm, one that often includes high notes of joy and, sometimes, the lower octaves of stress and societal pressures. This chapter is your cozy nook, a place to explore how to tune into your mental well-being and orchestrate a life that resonates with harmony and health for you and your entire family.

Mental Health Support for LGBTQ+ Parents

The mental load of parenting can sometimes feel like carrying a backpack filled with bricks—necessary but heavy. For LGBTQ+ parents, this backpack often comes with a few extra bricks. Societal discrimination, the nuances of navigating non-traditional family dynamics, and the ongoing dance for acceptance can add layers of stress that might feel overwhelming at times. Recognizing these unique stressors is the first step in lightening that load. Whether it's the sting of microaggressions at the school gate or the subtle tension of family gatherings, these experiences can slowly chip away at your mental peace.

Finding LGBTQ+ friendly mental health services can sometimes feel like searching for a needle in a haystack. It's crucial, however, to seek support from professionals who understand and affirm your family's identity. Start by consulting LGBTQ+ health centers or resources like the Gay and Lesbian Medical Association, which provides a directory of healthcare professionals specializing in LGBTQ+ care. Don't hesitate to ask potential therapists about their experience with LGBTQ+ issues during your initial consultation. Remember, the goal is to find someone who doesn't just "get it" but also cheers for your family's well-being.

Support groups and community resources can be incredible lifelines. These groups mirror your experiences, reflecting understanding and providing shared strategies for coping and thriving. Organizations like PFLAG and local LGBTQ+ community centers often run groups for parents, offering a space to vent, share, and support each other. Imagine walking into a room (or a Zoom call) where everyone not only understands your joke about your toddler's obsession with the non-binary unicorn plushie but also nods in understanding when you share your fears about future challenges.

Emotional regulation techniques are your secret tools for keeping the stress backpack manageable. Mindfulness, meditation, and therapeutic writing can help ground your thoughts and ease anxiety. Apps like Headspace offer guided meditation sessions that can be squeezed into your morning routine or before bed. Journaling can also be a powerful tool. Try setting aside a few minutes each day to jot down your thoughts, or maybe even share a journal with your partner, where you both can express your feelings and experiences. These practices aren't just about reducing stress at the moment but about building resilience for whatever melody life plays next.

Navigating the complexities of LGBTQ+ parenting requires more than just love and good intentions—it demands practical tools and informed strategies for mental well-being. By recognizing the unique stressors you face, seeking to affirm mental health support, leaning on the strength of community resources, and employing techniques to manage emotional stress, you set the stage for a healthier, happier family life. Remember, taking care of your mental health isn't a luxury; it's an essential part of being the best parent you can be. As you turn these pages, imagine them as stepping stones leading you toward a place where you feel supported, empowered, and understood, ready to face each day with confidence and joy.

Stress Management Techniques for Busy Parents

Ah, the symphony of life as an LGBTQ+ parent—sometimes it's sweet and harmonious, and other times, let's be real, it feels a bit more like a cacophony. Between juggling school runs, meal planning, and, oh yes, that thing called 'personal time,' finding balance can sometimes feel like spotting a unicorn in your backyard. But fear not, dear reader, for we've got some strategies up our sleeve that might help you orchestrate a more balanced, less stressful daily routine.

Let's talk time management, the conductor's baton of your daily life. Effective time management isn't just about squeezing every second out of your day; it's about creating a rhythm that allows you, your partner, and your kids to thrive. Start by visualizing your typical week—what are the non-negotiables? These might include work hours, school drop-offs, and downtime. Yes, penciling in 'do nothing' is not only allowed, it's encouraged. Once you've mapped out these basics, look for pockets of time slipping through the cracks. Perhaps it's the hour spent scrolling through social media (we've all been there), or it's time lost to inefficiency, like multiple weekly grocery trips. Consider batching similar tasks together—running all your errands in one swoop or meal prepping on Sundays—which can free up time throughout the week for more family fun or a quiet cup of coffee alone.

Now, let's move on to relaxation techniques because managing stress is as crucial as managing time. Integrating simple practices like deep breathing exercises can make a significant difference. Try this: inhale deeply for four counts, hold for four, exhale for four, and repeat. Simple, right? But oh, so effective, especially in those 'pulling my hair out' moments. Yoga and meditation are other fantastic tools. And no, you don't need to twist yourself into a pretzel or chant for hours. Yoga can be as simple as a few stretches in the morning to wake up the body and calm the mind. Many apps and online platforms offer short guided meditation sessions that can be squeezed into your morning routine or right before bed, helping to center your thoughts and ease anxiety.

Prioritizing self-care isn't just beneficial; it's essential, and yes, it goes beyond the occasional bubble bath (though those are nice, too). It's about finding what replenishes you and making it a non-negotiable part of your routine. Maybe it's a weekly jog, a craft project, or quiet time with a book—whatever fills your cup. Communicate with your partner about your self-care needs and listen to theirs. This mutual understanding can help ensure that both of you get the time you need to recharge, making you better partners and parents.

Lastly, let's remember the power of family activities in reducing stress. Whether hiking through a nearby trail, cycling around the neighborhood, or getting messy with some arts and crafts, these activities aren't just fun—they're bonding opportunities that strengthen your family's connection and create joyful memories. Plus, they're a great way to blow off steam and involve everyone in something that isn't screen-related. These moments of togetherness are the antidotes to the stresses of daily life, reminding you of what truly matters—time spent with those you love.

You can transform the overwhelming orchestra of your daily responsibilities into a more harmonious melody through smart time management, effective relaxation techniques, committed self-care, and engaging in family activities. It's about finding what works for your unique family rhythm and tweaking it as you go along because if there's anything we parents know, flexibility and a good sense of humor are key to getting through the day. So here's to less stress and more moments of joy and connection with your family. Remember, you're not just managing life; you're crafting the life you want to live, beat by beautiful beat.

Addressing Health Disparities: Advocating for LGBTQ+ Specific Care

Dealing with the healthcare system as an LGBTQ+ parent can be complicated and frustrating, but it's manageable with the right steps. Knowing the health disparities you might face helps you better prepare and handle the challenges. These disparities can range from higher rates of stress due to societal discrimination to less access to healthcare services that are culturally competent and affirming of LGBTQ+ identities. For instance, finding a pediatrician who is not only top-notch in their medical skills but also deeply understands and respects LGBTQ+ family dynamics can sometimes feel like hunting for a unicorn. These barriers are not just inconvenient; they can have profound impacts on both your and your children's well-being.

Advocating for more inclusive healthcare policies is your next step in this process. It's about making the system work adequately and excellently for your family. This advocacy can take many forms, from attending town hall meetings and speaking out about your needs to joining or forming advocacy groups focusing on LGBTQ+ health issues. Connecting with larger organizations such as the Human Rights Campaign or the National LGBTQ Task Force can amplify your voice. These groups often have the resources and networks to push for significant local, state, and national policy changes. For example, advocating for policies that require healthcare providers to undergo LGBTQ+ sensitivity and inclusivity training can make a substantial difference in the quality of care you and your family receive.

Creating an inclusive healthcare plan is like mapping your route through uncharted territory. It begins with understanding exactly what your family needs—from routine preventive care to possibly more complex medical services. One effective strategy is to develop a relationship with a healthcare provider who gets your family and becomes an advocate for you within the healthcare system. This might involve initial consultations with various providers to discuss your family's needs and gauge their understanding and support of LGBTQ+ health issues. Once you find the right match, work with them to create a healthcare plan that addresses all aspects of your family's health, ensuring that everyone gets the care they need when they need it, without judgment or discrimination.

Lastly, arming yourself with knowledge and resources to navigate the healthcare system effectively is like having the best navigation app on your phone during a road trip. Numerous organizations and online resources are dedicated to helping LGBTQ+ families like yours. The Gay and Lesbian Medical Association offers a directory of healthcare providers committed to ensuring LGBTQ+ individuals and families receive competent care. Websites like OutCare Health provide listings and reviews of LGBTQ+ friendly healthcare professionals across various specialties. Furthermore, consider connecting with local LGBTQ+ community centers, which often have partnerships with healthcare providers who are allies of the LGBTQ+ community and can be tremendous resources in your healthcare journey.

By addressing these disparities and advocating for inclusive care, you're helping your family and making things better for every LGBTQ+ family in the future. Each step you take builds a more inclusive, understanding, and compassionate healthcare system that recognizes and celebrates the diversity of families it serves. So, as you turn these pages and plan your next steps, know that with each move, you're creating a legacy of health and equity for your family and the entire LGBTQ+ community.

Building Resilience in LGBTQ+ Families

Resilience in LGBTQ+ families isn't just about bouncing back from challenges; it's about thriving amidst them, much like a garden that survives and flourishes even in the most unpredictable weather. For families like ours, resilience comes from understanding, support, and unconditional acceptance, helping us handle societal pressures and internal struggles. It allows us to stand firm when faced with discrimination or navigate the complex emotions that can arise within our family dynamics or external interactions.

Building this resilience begins at home with the stories we tell ourselves and each other about who we are and what we stand for. These narratives are powerful; they shape our perceptions and can be sources of strength or contribute to our stresses. Imagine framing your family's story to highlight strength, love, and diversity as sources of pride. Celebrate the unique aspects of your family by creating a family tree that includes biological and chosen family members, highlighting the diverse makeup of your family. This positive narrative reinforces to all family members the value of their personal and collective identities, fortifying self-esteem and unity.

Fostering open communication flows naturally from maintaining a positive family narrative. It involves creating an environment where everyone feels safe and valued in sharing their thoughts, feelings, and experiences. Regular family meetings can be a great forum for this, providing a dedicated space for discussing anything from daily happenings to more significant issues like experiences of discrimination or personal challenges. During these sessions, encourage each family member to express their difficulties, joys, and achievements. This practice supports individual emotional processing and enhances mutual understanding and collective problem-solving within the family.

Supporting each family member's individuality is another cornerstone of building resilience. This means recognizing and nurturing each person's unique interests, strengths, and challenges. It might involve supporting your child's interest in art or music, even if it's new territory for you, or embracing your partner's recent interest in volunteer work. By affirming each person's pursuits and passions, you reinforce their sense of self-worth and belonging within the family, which is crucial for personal resilience.

Community support plays a pivotal role in extending this resilience beyond the confines of home. Engaging with LGBTQ+ organizations can provide a broader support network that offers emotional backing, practical resources, and advocacy. These groups understand the specific challenges faced by LGBTQ+ families and can offer everything from legal advice and psychological support to family-friendly social events. Being part of such communities helps normalize your family's experiences, provides valuable learning opportunities, and can provide immense comfort and strength.

Case Studies of Resilient Families

Consider the case of Drew and Morgan, a couple with two children who faced significant opposition from extended family members due to their LGBTQ+ status. By consistently framing their family narrative around themes of love and resilience and openly discussing their challenges during family meetings, they fostered a strong sense of identity and solidarity in their children. They also became active members of an LGBTQ+ parenting group, which not only provided them with emotional support but also equipped them with strategies to handle familial opposition constructively.

Then there's the story of Jules, a non-binary parent who struggled initially with isolation in a conservative community. Through local LGBTQ+ advocacy groups, Jules found camaraderie and platforms for educating others about non-binary identities, enhancing their sense of purpose and community belonging. This involvement bolstered Jules' resilience and fostered an environment of inclusivity within their wider community circle.

Building resilience in LGBTQ+ families involves creating a strong network of stories, communication, individuality, and community to support and uplift each family member. By focusing on these areas, you ensure that your family isn't just surviving challenges but thriving through them, equipped with the love, understanding, and support necessary to navigate whatever life throws your way. This resilience is your legacy—a gift that empowers each family member to face the world with confidence and pride, no matter the circumstances.

The Role of Nutrition and Physical Health in Family Well-Being

Navigating the kitchen with your typical family hustle and bustle, you might find yourself wondering if you're feeding your family the best you can, especially when considering the unique nutritional needs that might come with being an LGBTQ+ family. You may be managing hormonal treatments that affect appetite or stress levels that skew your family's eating habits. It's like being a chef with a very specific recipe to follow —one that changes with each day's needs. Understanding these unique dietary considerations is crucial. For instance, certain hormone therapies might require protein intake adjustments or careful calorie intake monitoring. At the same time, managing stress might lead to prioritizing foods rich in omega-3 fatty acids, which are known to help regulate mood.

Planning healthy meals on a budget can sometimes feel like a high-wire act—balancing nutritional needs without breaking the bank. Begin by embracing the art of meal planning. It sounds tedious, but it can become an engaging family activity with a dash of creativity. Sit down weekly and draft a meal plan involving everyone in decision-making. This ensures that the meals are diverse, cater to everyone's dietary needs and prevent last-minute unhealthy choices. Bulk-buying staples like rice, beans, and frozen vegetables can be cost-effective and ensure you always have the basics. Incorporating meatless meals a few times a week can also reduce costs and introduce variety. Remember, healthy eating doesn't require exotic ingredients; simple, well-balanced meals can be nutritious and delicious.

Physical activity should be a cornerstone of family life, not just for maintaining physical health but also for bonding and improving mental health. Regular family activities, like biking on weekends, playing tag in the backyard, or even an evening walk after dinner, can significantly boost everyone's mood and overall health. These moments of activity are not just about exercise; they're about creating memories, sharing laughs, and blowing off the steam of daily life. For instance, organizing a weekly family soccer game can become a tradition everyone looks forward to, providing routine physical activity and a chance to connect without screens or distractions.

In terms of resources, a wealth of information can guide you in making informed choices about nutrition and fitness. Websites like ChooseMyPlate.gov offer personalized eating plans and tips on healthy eating based on the latest nutrition guidelines. For fitness, look for local community centers or LGBTQ+ friendly gyms that offer family memberships with diverse programs that can engage all family members. Online platforms like YouTube also have treasure troves of workout videos that can fit any schedule, from five-minute yoga sessions to family dance-offs in the living room. Incorporating good nutrition and fun physical activities into your family life promotes a healthy lifestyle beyond just meals and workouts, making wellness a part of your daily routine.

Self-care Strategies for Sustaining Healthy Family Relationships

Everyone—parent, child, or caregiver—is important in keeping things healthy and happy. For LGBTQ+ families, ensuring every member thrives individually and together is important. Creating individual self-care plans gives each person the space to grow and care for their unique needs.

Encouraging each family member to develop a self-care plan involves recognizing and respecting their needs and preferences. This might look like one child needing quiet time to read after school while another finds solace in loud, energetic play. One parent may find rejuvenation in weekly yoga classes, while another prefers journaling before bed. These personal rituals aren't selfish; they are essential for individual well-being, contributing to the family's overall health. When each person's needs are met, they are better equipped to engage positively with each other, reducing friction and enhancing harmony within the family.

Embedding communication as a form of self-care within the family structure is a preventive measure against misunderstandings and builds trust. Think of it as oiling the gears of a well-used machine; without it, things might grind to a halt under the pressure. Regular family meetings can be an excellent venue, providing a structured opportunity for everyone to share their thoughts, feelings, and needs. These meetings should be approached openly and non-judgmentally, ensuring that all voices are heard and valued. This practice not only clears up misunderstandings but also reinforces the support network within the family, making each member feel supported and connected.

Balancing the demands of parenting with personal growth activities is crucial for maintaining one's sense of self and preventing burnout. It's easy to get caught up in the role of 'parent' and forget that you are also an individual with dreams, hobbies, and interests. Encouraging personal growth activities, such as pursuing a new hobby, continuing education, or dedicating time to a long-lost passion, can rejuvenate one's spirit and enhance overall life satisfaction. This balance benefits the individual and sets a positive example for children, showing them that personal development is lifelong. When children see their parents prioritizing personal growth, they learn to value and pursue their interests and passions.

Modeling effective self-care behaviors for children is one of the most direct ways to instill healthy habits they can carry into adulthood. Children learn by example, and when they see their parents actively engaging in self-care practices, they understand their value. This might include involving children in your exercise routine, showing them how you manage stress through meditation or inviting them to participate in planning and cooking healthy meals. By integrating these practices into daily life, children absorb these habits naturally. This prepares them to manage their well-being as they grow and normalize self-care as a regular part of life, not just a stress response.

In nurturing each family member's well-being through personalized self-care plans, open communication, balancing parenting with personal growth, and modeling healthy behaviors, LGBTQ+ families can cultivate a thriving environment. Each of these strategies intertwines to strengthen the family unit, ensuring that each member not only survives the challenges of daily life but thrives amidst them. As you incorporate these practices into your family life, remember that each small effort adds to your family's overall strength and happiness, making it resilient and vibrant.

As we wrap up this chapter on health and well-being, it's clear that nurturing individual health, fostering open communication, and embracing a balanced approach to family and personal life are beneficial and essential strategies for sustaining healthy relationships within LGBTQ+ families.

These practices ensure that every family member can confidently navigate life's challenges, supported by love and mutual respect. As we move forward, the lessons and strategies outlined here pave the way for building stronger, more resilient family units that stand ready to face the future, whatever it may hold.

SEVEN

Legal and Advocacy Considerations

Imagine you're preparing for a big road trip across the country—you'd need to know the road conditions, speed limits, and maybe some scenic stops along the way, right? Similarly, when navigating the landscape of LGBTQ+ parenting, staying informed about the legal terrain is crucial. It's not just about knowing the laws as they stand but keeping an ear to the ground for the rumblings of change that might affect your family's journey.

Staying Informed on Changing Laws Affecting LGBTQ+ Families

Keeping up with legal changes that could impact your family might not be the most exciting task, but think of it as your GPS—it helps you navigate and plan to avoid potential bumps on the road. One effective way to stay updated is by subscribing to legal newsletters focusing on LGBTQ+ issues. Organizations like the Human Rights Campaign (HRC) and Lambda Legal offer updates and analyses that break down complex legal lingo into bite-sized, easy-to-understand pieces.

You might wonder, "But how different can laws be across states?" Well, quite a bit! The landscape of LGBTQ+ family rights in America can vary dramatically from one state to another. For instance, some states have robust protections and recognition for LGBTQ+ parents, while others may have restrictive laws that could impact everything from adoption rights to parental recognition. This patchwork of laws affects those looking to become parents and those moving or traveling between states.

Understanding these differences is crucial. It's like knowing which roads are toll-free and which ones aren't—it helps you plan better and avoid unexpected detours. For example, if you're considering moving from California to a state with more restrictive laws, knowing the legal landscape can help you prepare for changes in how your family might be recognized or what steps you might need to take to safeguard your parental rights.

The impact of legal changes on LGBTQ+ families can be profound. Let's say a new law is passed that affects second-parent adoption procedures—a case study involving a family who underwent these changes can provide both insights and practical advice. These real-life examples highlight the direct effects of legal changes and offer strategies on how families navigated these challenges, offering a roadmap for others in similar situations.

Compiling a list of websites, blogs, and organizations where you can access reliable and timely information on legal issues is invaluable for those who like to have resources at their fingertips. Websites like the ACLU's LGBT Rights section or blogs like Mombian, which offers parenting news and tips with an LGBTQ+ focus, can be great resources. They provide legal news, practical advice, and community support, helping you stay informed and connected.

Navigating the legal landscape as an LGBTQ+ parent or prospective parent is like a captain charting a course through ever-changing waters. It requires vigilance, preparedness, and a good map—or, in this case, reliable resources and a support network. By staying informed, understanding the variations in state and federal laws, and learning from the experiences of those who have navigated these waters before, you can steer your family through with confidence, ensuring that no matter how the legal winds may shift, you're ready to adjust your sails and keep moving forward toward a secure and joyful family life.

Advocacy and Legal Challenges: Fighting for Parental Rights

Stepping up to advocate for parental rights can feel like gearing up for a superhero mission, where your cape is your unwavering determination, and your powers are your voice and actions. Within LGBTQ+ parenting, your advocacy can take many forms, from sharing your family's story to influence hearts and minds to engaging in more formal actions like litigation or policy advocacy. Each form of advocacy plays a crucial role in shaping a more just and inclusive society for LGBTQ+ families.

Imagine starting with grassroots campaign advocacy from the ground up. It's about creating waves in your immediate community that eventually spread outward. This could look like organizing local events that raise awareness about LGBTQ+ parental rights or setting up booths at fairs and community gatherings to distribute information and gather support. Social media also offers a powerful platform to amplify your voice. By creating compelling content that highlights the challenges and triumphs of LGBTQ+ parenting, you can spark conversations, connect with others in similar situations, and mobilize a community of advocates. Remember, change often starts with a single voice that dares to speak out, slowly drawing in a chorus of others.

Now, let's talk about litigation. The fight for parental rights sometimes requires legal battles, where the courtroom becomes the arena. Engaging in litigation can be daunting, but it's a necessary tool when policies directly infringe upon your rights as an LGBTQ+ parent. For example, challenging state laws that may deny a non-biological parent the rights to their child can pave the way for broader legal recognition of diverse family structures. These battles aren't just about winning a case; they're about setting precedents that will protect other families in the future.

Engaging with policymakers is where you take the conversation directly to those who can make or break laws affecting LGBTQ+ families. Effective engagement can range from writing letters and making phone calls to legislators to more direct interactions like participating in hearings or legislative sessions. When writing to a lawmaker, your story is your most powerful tool. Personalize your correspondence, explain how specific laws or policies affect your family personally, and articulate clearly what changes you hope to see. Remember, lawmakers are there to represent you, so let them know exactly how they can do that.

Building coalitions with other advocacy groups can significantly amplify your efforts. Whether it's LGBTQ+ rights organizations, parenting groups, or civil rights entities, these alliances can pool resources, knowledge, and influence, making your advocacy efforts stronger and more impactful. Forming these coalitions often starts with reaching out to organizations with aligned goals, attending the same events, or inviting them to collaborate on specific campaigns. The unity and solidarity in these coalitions bolster your advocacy efforts and foster a sense of community and shared purpose that can sustain you through the challenges of fighting for legal change.

Navigating the maze of legal challenges and advocacy efforts is no small feat, but remember, every step you take builds the path toward a more inclusive world for LGBTQ+ parents and their children. Whether you're sharing your story at a local school, challenging unfair laws in court, or sitting down with policymakers, your actions come together to form the larger story of progress and perseverance in the fight for equality. So, put on that metaphorical cape, and let's continue to push for a future where all families are recognized, respected, and celebrated.

International Travel: Navigating Different Legal Landscapes as an LGBTQ+ Family

Packing your bags for an international adventure often comes with a mix of excitement and a bit of anxiety—especially when you're traveling as an LGBTQ+ family. There's more to consider than what swimsuit to pack or landmarks to visit. Ensuring you're prepared legally can be as crucial as remembering your passport. Before setting foot on that plane, ensure you have your legal ducks in a row. This means ensuring that all travel documents are up-to-date and accurately reflect each family member's legal status, including names and gender markers if applicable. Obtaining the right visas is crucial, as is carrying documentation that establishes parental rights and relationships, especially for non-biological parents. In some countries, showing proof of your relationship with your child can be as routine as a security check.

Understanding the legal status of LGBTQ+ families in your destination country is like checking the weather—you need to know what you're walking into. This preparation can range from understanding mild legal nuances to preparing for potential heavy storms. For instance, while countries like Canada or the Netherlands offer a warm welcome, others may pose significant challenges due to restrictive laws and practices. Before traveling, a good practice is to consult travel advisories from reliable sources like the International Lesbian, Gay, Bisexual, Trans and Intersex Association (ILGA), which provides up-to-date information on the legal situation for LGBTQ+ individuals by country. This research can help you avoid places where your family might face legal difficulties or danger.

Now, let's move on to the risks and how to mitigate them. It's not just about knowing which countries have restrictive laws but understanding how they could affect your family. For instance, if a country has laws that criminalize homosexuality, even actions perceived as benign, such as checking into a hotel room with your spouse, could potentially lead to issues. In such cases, it might be wise to reconsider your travel plans or at least prepare meticulously by understanding your legal rights and having a backup plan. This might include booking accommodations that are known to be LGBTQ+ friendly or using a travel agency that specializes in LGBTQ+ travel.

Emergency planning is your safety net. It's like having a good insurance policy—you hope you never need to use it, but it's indispensable when the unexpected happens. Always have the contact information for your country's embassy or consulate within easy reach. These can be vital resources in a crisis, from replacing lost passports to interceding with local authorities if you face legal challenges. Additionally, knowing the contact details of local LGBTQ+ organizations or international legal aid services that can assist if your rights are challenged can be a lifeline in times of need.

Cultural sensitivity and awareness go a long way in ensuring that your travels are safe and enjoyable. Every country has its cultural norms and practices, and being aware of these can help you navigate social situations more smoothly. This doesn't mean you must compromise who you are, but understanding and respecting local customs can enhance your travel experience and help avoid unnecessary complications. For instance, in some cultures, public displays of affection are frowned upon, regardless of sexual orientation. Being mindful of such nuances can help you blend in and enjoy your journey more peacefully.

Navigating international travel as an LGBTQ+ family requires extra planning and consideration. Yet, with the right preparations—legal and otherwise—you can embark on your family adventure with a greater sense of security and freedom. Whether you're exploring ancient ruins, enjoying exotic beaches, or experiencing vibrant cultures, the world has an incredible amount to offer. By taking these steps, you ensure that your family can experience it fully, safely, and joyfully.

Estate Planning and Future Security for LGBTQ+ Families

Consider estate planning a bit like setting up a safety net under a trapeze act—it's there to ensure everything goes smoothly, no matter what happens during the performance. For LGBTQ+ families, this safety net is crucial, not just to manage assets but to provide a secure future for children and protect the rights of non-biological parents. The reality is that without a clear, legally sound estate plan, the people you love most could face unnecessary complications at a time when they're most vulnerable.

Estate planning involves a few key elements that help safeguard your family's future. First up, let's talk about wills and trusts. A will is your basic "who gets what" document—it outlines how you want your assets distributed after you pass away and can specify guardians for your children. Trusts, on the other hand, offer more control over how your assets are managed and distributed. They can be particularly handy for ensuring that funds are available to your children when they need them, perhaps for education or healthcare, and can be structured to provide financial support over a period of time.

Healthcare directives and powers of attorney are just as important, particularly for LGBTQ+ families. These documents ensure that your wishes regarding medical treatment are respected and designate who can decide on your behalf if you cannot do so yourself. This can be crucial in emergencies, where non-biological parents might not automatically be recognized as next of kin. Imagine a situation where you're unable to make medical decisions for yourself, and your partner, who knows your wishes better than anyone, is legally sidelined. Proper documentation prevents this, ensuring that the person you trust most is making those critical decisions.

For non-traditional families, these legal tools are not just useful but essential. They help navigate the complexities that might not affect heterosexual or biological family structures. For instance, ensuring that assets pass according to your wishes might involve setting up special provisions in your will or trust, especially if your family includes step-children or you're not married to your partner. Similarly, protecting the rights of non-biological parents might mean setting up trusts that provide for the child but also stipulate access or guardianship in line with your family's needs.

Finding the right attorney to help you navigate this process is like finding the right coach for your trapeze act—they need to know the ropes and guide you through the routine flawlessly. Look for an attorney who specializes in estate planning for LGBTQ+ families. They will be familiar with the unique challenges and legal nuances you might face. When you meet potential candidates, ask questions about their experience with similar families, their approach to complex family structures, and their strategy for protecting your rights and wishes. Their answers should indicate their ability to handle your family's specific needs effectively.

Estate planning is more than just a legal task; it's an act of love. It's about ensuring that the people you care about are cared for, even when you're not there to do it yourself. By setting up a comprehensive estate plan, you're not just securing assets; you're providing peace of mind and securing a legacy that respects and protects your family's unique structure and needs. With the right plans, you can rest a little easier, knowing that your safety net is strong, comprehensive, and tailored to hold your family securely, no matter what life throws your way.

The Role of Legal Advocates and How to Engage Them

Imagine navigating a thick forest — it's beautiful but challenging, and having a skilled guide can make all the difference. That's what engaging a legal advocate feels like when traversing the intricate landscape of LGBTQ+ family law. Legal advocates are your guides, equipped with the expertise to help you manage the legal thickets you might encounter, from adoption proceedings and discrimination cases to gender marker changes on official documents. These professionals range from lawyers representing you in court to legal advisors who help decipher complex laws to lobbyists advocating for policy changes benefiting LGBTQ+ families. Their role is multifaceted, adapting to the terrain of your specific legal needs.

When should you consider bringing a legal advocate into your family's life? Think of it like deciding when to call in a plumber. Sometimes, you might manage fine with your trusty tool kit; other times, you need a pro. Engaging a legal advocate is wise during any process where the stakes are high, and the law is complex. For instance, a legal advocate can be invaluable if you adopt a child and navigate the intersecting laws of state, federal, and possibly international jurisdictions. They ensure that all paperwork is flawless, deadlines are met, and your rights as an LGBTQ+ parent are vigorously defended. Similarly, in discrimination cases, whether you're facing unfair treatment at work due to your family structure or your child is experiencing bias in school, a legal advocate can help you understand your rights and craft a strategy to address these issues effectively.

Working with legal advocates requires clear communication — it's a bit like conducting an orchestra. Each party needs to know the score and how to play their parts perfectly. Start by being upfront about your expectations and the specifics of your case. Keep all lines of communication open and regular, updating your advocate on any new developments and vice versa. Understanding some of the legal jargon that flies around in these conversations is crucial. Don't hesitate to ask for clarifications — no question is too small, and ensuring you fully understand each step of the process is key to a successful partnership. Remember, a good legal advocate doesn't just speak on your behalf; they empower you by demystifying the complexities of the law.

Finding trustworthy legal advocates well-versed in LGBTQ+ issues can sometimes feel like searching for a beacon in the fog. Start with LGBTQ+ community centers, often with directories of LGBTQ+-friendly legal professionals. Additionally, organizations such as the National Center for Lesbian Rights (NCLR) or Lambda Legal can provide referrals to reliable advocates experienced in handling cases for LGBTQ+ families. Online platforms like Avvo or the Martindale-Hubbell law directory allow you to search for attorneys by specialty and location while providing reviews and ratings. When choosing an advocate, consider their experience with similar cases, their approach to LGBTQ+ issues, and their overall philosophy towards family law. It's about finding someone who not only understands the law but also understands your family.

Creating Legacies: How LGBTQ+ Families are Shaping the Future

Imagine each step you take in advocacy and sharing your story as planting a seed for a garden that your children and their children will continue cultivating—a garden of rights, respect, and recognition. LGBTQ+ families, by their very presence and participation in the legal and social spheres, are reshaping not just the laws but the cultural narratives around family and identity. Whether a court case is fought, a law changed, or even a personal story is shared publicly, each action contributes to a broader shift toward inclusivity and equality.

The impact of these efforts on legislation and social norms is profound and far-reaching. Consider how recent changes in laws regarding marriage equality and parental rights have created waves of change across the globe. These changes didn't happen in a vacuum—they were driven by the tireless efforts of individuals and families who stood up and demanded recognition. Their victories reshape the legal landscape and transform societal perceptions, making it increasingly normal to see LGBTQ+ families represented in media, literature, and public life. It's a reinforcing cycle: as laws change, societal norms shift, fostering a more accepting environment that can lead to further legal advancements.

Stories of influence and change often start on a personal level, but their ripple effects can be monumental. Take, for example, a lesbian couple who challenged their local school district's policies to ensure their child could have the same rights as other children. Their fight not only led to a change in that district but also set a precedent that other schools followed. Or consider the trans man who successfully lobbied for a change in his state's policy on birth certificates, making it easier for trans parents to be correctly listed as their child's parent. These stories are not just inspiring—they're instructive. They show the strategies used, like forming alliances with civil rights organizations or harnessing the power of media, and the outcomes achieved, such as policy changes and increased public awareness.

Encouraging active participation among readers is essential. Think about what legacy you want to leave. Is it a world where LGBTQ+ families are fully recognized and valued? If so, your involvement is crucial. This can be as simple as voting for policies that support LGBTQ+ rights, participating in local LGBTQ+ organizations, or more involved measures like lobbying your representatives or sharing your family's story in public forums. Every action counts, and when collectively harnessed, these actions can lead to substantial changes.

Building a supportive community for future generations hinges on our actions today. It involves creating networks that not only support LGBTQ+ families but also educate the broader community. This support network can be the backbone for enduring change, providing the resources, emotional support, and advocacy needed to advance LGBTQ+ rights. It's about laying down a foundation of knowledge, support, and respect that each new generation can build upon, ensuring the rights and recognitions fought for today are preserved and enhanced in the future.

In closing this chapter, remember that the legacies we create through our actions today will echo through generations. Each step taken towards advocacy, each story shared, and each community strengthened contributes to a future where LGBTQ+ families are recognized not as exceptions but as equals. As we turn our sights to the next chapter, we carry forward this commitment to action, advocacy, and community building, ready to face new challenges and achieve new victories for LGBTQ+ families everywhere.

EIGHT

Stories of Pride and Joy

Personal Narratives: Single LGBTQ+ Parents Share Their Journeys

Parenting, with its unpredictable blend of challenges and triumphs, often feels like assembling an IKEA bookshelf without the instruction manual—particularly if you're doing it solo. Yet, many single LGBTQ+ parents assemble the shelf and turn it into a magnificent library, echoing with stories of resilience, love, and the unique joy of raising a child on your terms. In this chapter, we delve into the lives of single LGBTQ+ parents who have navigated the complexities of parenting solo, turning societal stigmas and logistical challenges into stepping stones toward fulfilling family lives.

Take James, for example, a single trans man who chose to become a parent through IVF. Navigating the medical system posed its own set of challenges, from selecting a donor to finding a fertility clinic that respected his identity and understood his needs. Despite the hurdles, the moment he held his daughter for the first time, every obstacle became worthwhile. His journey underscores not just the possibilities of modern reproductive technologies for LGBTQ+ individuals but also the importance of perseverance and self-advocacy in the face of systemic challenges.

Then there's Maria, who adopted her son, Nico, from foster care. As a single lesbian in a predominantly conservative community, she faced whispers and sideways glances at PTA meetings and soccer games. However, Maria turned these challenges into opportunities for advocacy, educating those around her about LGBTQ+ families. Her story is a testament to the power of visibility and the impact of sharing one's truth in fostering understanding and acceptance. Through community engagement and by forming close bonds with other LGBTQ+ parents in her area, Maria built a network of support that not only bolstered her parenting journey but also created a sense of extended family for Nico.

Support networks, as Maria discovered, are crucial. They can be a lifeline in moments of doubt and a source of celebration in times of joy. These networks might include fellow LGBTQ+ parents, allies, or family members who affirm and support your parenting journey. For single parents like Ryan, who found himself struggling to balance his career and his responsibilities as a father, it was a local LGBTQ+ parenting group that provided not only practical advice but also emotional support. This network became his village, assisting with everything from emergency childcare to navigating parent-teacher conferences.

The empowering messages from these narratives are clear: single LGBTQ+ parenting is not just about overcoming challenges;

it's about redefining what family looks like and embracing the journey with all its complexities. Whether through biological means, adoption, or fostering, these parents demonstrate that love, resilience, and community can create family dynamics as rich and fulfilling as any other. Their stories are not just instructional; they're inspirational, providing hope and encouragement for prospective single parents within the LGBTQ+ community. These narratives shine a light on the joys and fulfillments of raising children independently, celebrating the strength it takes to build a family on one's terms.

Through these stories, we see that the journey of single LGBTQ+ parenting, like any great story, is filled with moments of tension and triumph. But more importantly, it's underscored by an overwhelming amount of love—the kind that builds bridges, breaks down barriers, and paints a future rich with potential. For every single LGBTQ+ parent out there and those considering this path, these narratives are a reminder that while the road might be tough, it's also lined with moments of incredible joy and profound fulfillment.

Stories from Polyamorous Families: Challenges and Successes

Imagine a household where the weekly schedule looks more like a carefully orchestrated symphony than a mere calendar. Here, multiple partners share meals and living spaces and the intricate dance of co-parenting. This is the reality for many polyamorous families, a dynamic where love doesn't just double but multiplies, creating a unique set of joys and challenges. In these families, navigating the complexities of multiple adult relationships alongside parenting roles requires communication that would make even the most seasoned diplomat pause. Take the case of Brett, Remy, and Spencer, a triad who share a home and the responsibility of raising two energetic toddlers. Their success in managing this complex relationship structure is rooted deeply in open, honest communication. Weekly family meetings are their norm, where everything from household chores to emotional needs is discussed openly. This ongoing dialogue ensures that no one feels overlooked and that each adult's relationship with the children is respected and nurtured.

However, the harmony of polyamorous family life often meets with discordant notes from the outside world. Legal recognition, or the lack thereof, poses a significant hurdle. In many regions, laws are rigidly structured around monogamous, two-parent frameworks, leaving polyamorous families in a precarious position. For instance, if one parent needs to make medical decisions for a child or wants to enroll them in school, lacking a legal parental status can turn these simple acts into complex legal battles. Social acceptance is another battlefield. Polyamorous families frequently encounter misconceptions and judgments from their communities, which can isolate them and even impact their children. Despite these obstacles, families like Brett, Remy, and Spencer find ways to forge paths toward recognition and acceptance, often becoming inadvertent advocates for the visibility and rights of polyamorous families.

The triumphs of effective co-parenting in these settings are both inspiring and instructive. Consider a scenario where one partner excels in academic support while another shines in emotional coaching. Children in these families benefit from diverse perspectives and skills, which can lead to a more rounded upbringing. Success stories abound, where children raised in polyamorous families excel in environments that celebrate diversity and inclusivity, thanks to the varied support system at home. These stories not only challenge societal norms but also highlight the potential benefits of polyamorous family structures, where the adage 'it takes a village to raise a child' is lived out in vivid color.

Community integration plays a crucial role in the well-being of polyamorous families. By engaging with broader community structures, from schools and neighborhoods to online forums, these families can foster understanding and support for their unique dynamics. For example, by participating in community events and openly sharing their family structure, polyamorous families like that of Brett, Remy, and Spencer create opportunities for dialogue, decreasing stigma and increasing support. This integration benefits the adults and their children, who see their family structure reflected and respected in the wider community.

Navigating the intricate dynamics of polyamorous family life, facing legal and social challenges head-on, and celebrating the triumphs of a diverse family structure are all threads in the rich tapestry of polyamorous parenting. These families redefine what it means to be a family and highlight the boundless capacity of love and cooperation. Their stories are a testament to the resilience and richness that can flourish when people come together to build a life not bound by convention but woven from the heart.

Trans and Non-Binary Parenting Experiences

Navigating the world as a trans or non-binary parent comes with unique experiences that intertwine identity, expression, and parenting in challenging and incredibly enriching ways.

Picture this: you're at the playground, and a casual conversation with another parent shifts towards family dynamics. Here, you find a moment to share and educate, gently expanding someone's understanding of gender diversity. This is just a snapshot of the day-to-day life where trans and non-binary individuals raise their children and navigate their identities, often breaking new ground in societal norms and family structures.

For trans parents, the intersection of transitioning and parenting can be complex. Consider Cameron, a trans woman who began her transition after her daughter was born. Cameron's journey brought forth challenges, such as securing gender-affirming care while managing the responsibilities of parenthood. Health care, a universal concern, assumes a specific gravity here. Accessing knowledgeable and empathetic healthcare providers is crucial for the transitioning parent and supporting the child's understanding and adjustment to their parent's transition. Cameron had to advocate for herself repeatedly, ensuring her medical needs were met without compromising her parenting duties. Her story highlights the importance of resilience and self-advocacy, qualities that she's keen on passing down to her daughter.

Legal navigation is another critical aspect. Trans and non-binary parents often face legal hurdles related to their parental rights, especially if their legal gender does not align with societal expectations. Navigating these legal waters often requires a detailed understanding of local laws and, sometimes, the strategic use of legal services to ensure one's parental rights are protected and recognized. For instance, Pat, a non-binary parent, found themselves embroiled in a custody battle that questioned their role as a parent simply because their gender identity did not conform to traditional norms. Pat could affirm their parental rights through community support and legal assistance, setting a precedent that benefited their case and contributed to broader legal recognition for non-binary and trans parents.

Community support plays a pivotal role in the lives of trans and non-binary parents. It offers a buffer against societal challenges and a platform for sharing experiences and resources. Many find solace and strength in online communities and local support groups where they can connect with others who understand their journey. These spaces often provide emotional support and practical advice on everything from healthcare to legal issues, creating a network that empowers parents to navigate their unique paths more effectively.

When it comes to raising children with an awareness of gender diversity, trans and non-binary parents are uniquely positioned to foster an environment of openness and inclusivity. They can provide firsthand insights into gender fluidity, helping their children understand and respect diversity from a young age. This education is not just about gender but about embracing differences broadly, fostering empathy, and challenging stereotypes. Parents like Pat, who identifies as non-binary, use everyday moments to discuss gender with their children, integrating these lessons into storytime, play, and daily interactions. This ongoing conversation helps to normalize diversity, preparing their children to navigate a world where gender is understood beyond binary terms.

In these narratives, the resilience, creativity, and advocacy of trans and non-binary parents shine through. They are navigating the personal intersection of parenting and identity and pioneering new understandings of family and community. Their stories are essential, not just for other trans and non-binary individuals but for all parents and families engaged in the beautiful, complex task of raising the next generation in a world rich with diversity.

The Joys of Raising Children in a Two-Mom or Two-Dad Family

Imagine a household where the morning routine is a tag-team affair, and bedtime stories are a double feature—this is everyday life in many two-mom and two-dad households. The dynamics of dual-parent LGBTQ+ families often bring a richness that is both challenging and wonderfully rewarding. From the division of diaper duties to navigating school functions, these families create a parenting tag team about balance and support.

Take Lisa and Janet, for example, who have twins. While Lisa prepares breakfast each morning, Janet prepares the kids for school. This seamless division of labor isn't just about efficiency; it's about each mom playing to her strengths and supporting each other's weaknesses. This mutual support extends beyond daily routines into emotional territories, providing their children with a dual source of comfort and guidance. The presence of two engaged parents can mean double the support during tough times, such as dealing with school bullying or the emotional turmoil of teenage years. This dual support system helps children feel exceptionally secure and loved, knowing they have not one but two dedicated cheerleaders on their sideline, ready to face whatever life throws their way.

However, life isn't always a smooth ride. External misconceptions about LGBTQ+ family structures can sometimes cast shadows over the joy. Whether it's the assumption that their kids lack a male or female role model or misguided queries about the 'real' parent, two-mom and two-dad families often debunk myths. But here's where the magic happens: these challenges become teachable moments for their children, teachers, peers, and the community. By openly discussing their family structure, parents like Lisa and Janet turn misconceptions into opportunities for education and dialogue, fostering a broader understanding of what family can mean. This proactive approach helps their children develop confidence in their family identity, equipping them with the resilience and pride to handle and educate others about their family dynamics.

Building strong bonds within these families goes beyond the walls of their homes; it extends into their neighborhoods and communities. In many cases, two-mom and two-dad households become inadvertent community leaders, spearheading initiatives like neighborhood inclusivity events or LGBTQ+ awareness programs in local schools. Their active involvement often positions these families as integral parts of their communities, enhancing visibility and support for LGBTQ+ families. It's not just about advocacy; it's about creating a community environment where diversity is accepted and celebrated.

Community engagement often leads to advocacy, as these families find themselves at the forefront of pushing for greater acceptance and rights for LGBTQ+ parents and their children. Through efforts like participating in school boards, contributing to local LGBTQ+ organizations, or even engaging in legislative advocacy, two-mom and two-dad families are not just raising children; they're raising awareness, shifting paradigms, and paving the way for future generations of LGBTQ+ families. This blend of personal joy in raising their children and their broader impact within their communities creates a legacy of love, resilience, and change.

In every shared bedtime story, every school meeting attended, and every community event organized, two-mom and two-dad families are redefining the narratives of parenting and family life. They show that love, respect, and commitment are the most crucial ingredients in the family recipe, irrespective of whether a family has a mom and a dad, two moms, or two dads. These families remind us that while the structure may differ, the content—love and care—remains the same, offering a powerful testament to the beauty of diversity in family life.

Lessons Learned: Veteran LGBTQ+ Parents Offer Advice

When you sit down with veteran LGBTQ+ parents who have navigated the parenting paths from diapers to diplomas, there's a wealth of wisdom to uncover that often feels like a treasure trove of "what I wish I knew" and "what worked for us." These seasoned parents have witnessed first-hand the shifts in societal attitudes towards LGBTQ+ families over decades, and their experiences provide invaluable insights for new or prospective parents within the community. They've seen the landscape change from when legal protections were sparse and societal acceptance was even sparser to today's increasingly inclusive—but still challenging—environment.

Reflecting on these shifts, veteran parents like Michael and John, who raised their daughter Sarah in the 90s, recall the necessity of creating safe, affirming spaces within their home and finding community support that wasn't always readily available. They had to be pioneers, often navigating without much precedent, but their efforts helped lay the groundwork for the rights and recognitions newer LGBTQ+ parents might experience today. They emphasize how different regions can vary, like a patchwork quilt regarding acceptance and legal rights, highlighting the importance of local community resources and legal advocacy if you're considering moving or traveling.

Advice from these parents often centers on the cornerstone of resilience. They advocate for building a robust personal and communal support system, emphasizing that this network is crucial for the tough times and celebrating the victories. Resilience, they note, doesn't mean going it alone; it means knowing when to lean on friends, family, or local support groups and how to foster resilience in your children. They share stories like organizing informal family gatherings that grew into larger community celebrations, where children could see other families like theirs and feel a part of a larger tapestry.

Moreover, these parents are staunch advocates for ongoing advocacy, not just in the big, headline-making ways but in everyday interactions that challenge stereotypes and educate others. They encourage new parents to engage in whatever form of advocacy feels right for them, whether participating in school boards, writing op-eds, or simply living openly and authentically. Their stories underscore advocacy as a powerful tool for change, shaping societal attitudes and forging better paths for future LGBTQ+ families.

Passing on legacies of pride, resilience, and advocacy to the next generation is perhaps the most heartfelt advice veteran LGBTQ+ parents offer. They speak about the importance of instilling a sense of pride in their children about their family structure and how this pride becomes a shield against discrimination and a source of strength. They talk about the conversations they've had, the family traditions they've created that celebrate their uniqueness, and the ways they've involved their children in advocacy, imparting the importance of standing up not only for their rights but for the rights of others.

In these narratives, there is a profound sense of passing the torch, of ensuring that the struggles and triumphs of yesterday's and today's LGBTQ+ parents pave the way for a brighter, more inclusive tomorrow. Through their stories, these veteran parents offer a roadmap filled with practical advice and heartfelt encouragement. They inspire a vision of a world where all families are celebrated for the love they share, not the labels they carry. Their legacy is one of enduring strength and boundless love, a reminder that while the landscape of LGBTQ+ parenting continues to evolve, the foundation built on resilience, advocacy, and pride stands firm, guiding the next generation of parents and children alike.

Celebrating Community: How LGBTQ+ Families Build and Sustain Joy

Picture a vibrant festival where families of all shapes and colors come together, laughter bubbling over like a pot on the stove, streamers flying high. This is the essence of community-centered celebrations that many LGBTQ+ families partake in. These events bring us joy and help us feel more connected to our communities. Take, for instance, the annual Pride picnic hosted in a small town, where LGBTQ+ families and allies gather to share food, stories, and games. Kids dash around with rainbow flags, parents exchange parenting tips over lemonade, and everyone can feel part of a larger family. Such celebrations strengthen bonds among community members and create a space where joy and acceptance are abundantly clear. They serve as powerful reminders to LGBTQ+ families that they are not alone and that their love and lives are celebrated and supported by a community that values diversity.

Community organizations play a pivotal role in orchestrating these joyous occasions. From planning Pride parades to organizing family-friendly workshops and support groups, these organizations provide resources and safe spaces where LGBTQ+ families can connect and flourish. For example, a local LGBTQ+ center might run an annual summer camp explicitly designed for LGBTQ+ families, offering activities that are inclusive and affirming of all family structures. These organizations act as the glue that holds the community together, continually finding new ways to support and enrich the lives of LGBTQ+ families. Their efforts ensure that these families have access to a network of support that understands their unique challenges and celebrates their diverse experiences.

Stories of inclusion and support often stem from these community networks, illustrating the profound impact of solidarity on family well-being. Imagine a transgender parent who feels isolated in their parenting journey, finding a support group through a community organization. Here, they connect with other LGBTQ+ parents, sharing experiences and advice, and slowly, the isolation melts away, replaced by a sense of belonging and confidence. These stories are not just heartwarming; they're vital. They provide hope and a roadmap for other LGBTQ+ families seeking community and understanding. They show that within these communities, families can find acceptance and a collective strength that uplifts each member.

Creating spaces for joy involves active participation from LGBTQ+ families and the broader community. It's about more than attending events; it's about contributing to creating these spaces. Families might volunteer at local LGBTQ+ festivals, help organize community meetings, or simply show up and participate in community discussions. Each action, no matter how small, helps to foster a culture of inclusion and celebration. It's a proactive approach to community building, where every family contributes to the atmosphere of acceptance and support.

As LGBTQ+ families continue to navigate their unique paths, the community's role in nurturing and sustaining joy remains invaluable. Through celebrations, support from community organizations, shared stories of inclusion, and active participation in creating joyful spaces, these families strengthen their bonds and affirm their rightful place in society. Engaging in these community activities allows families to experience joy and multiply it, spreading it throughout their communities and beyond, ensuring that the echoes of their laughter and love are heard far and wide.

In wrapping up this exploration of community and joy within LGBTQ+ families, it's clear that the strength of these families is amplified through their connections with each other and their allies. From vibrant celebrations to the quiet support offered in group meetings, the community plays a crucial role in ensuring that every LGBTQ+ family can thrive in an environment that embraces diversity and fosters joy. These themes of resilience, support, and celebration carry with us, reminding us of the powerful community bond and the endless capacity for joy within the LGBTQ+ family experience.

NINE

Conclusion

W e are at the end of our shared journey through 'LGBTQ+ Parents Guide to Raising Kids With Pride.' We've navigated a lot together—from unpacking the diverse options for family-building like adoption, surrogacy, and biological parenting to tackling the often-daunting legal landscapes that affect our families. We've shared stories and strategies that foster community support and celebrated the joys, love, and sometimes the rollercoaster ride of LGBTQ+ parenting.

Throughout this book, I've aimed to empower you and your family with the knowledge and practical strategies that reinforce a strong sense of belonging. It's been about equipping us with the tools to cope and thrive, building resilient families that stand strong in the face of challenges. We've delved into the importance of staying updated with legal knowledge and the necessity of advocating for our rights, ensuring that we're not just surviving but paving the way for easier journeys for those who follow.

Community and chosen family—these concepts have surfaced repeatedly, haven't they? We've seen how vital a supportive network is for tough times and beautiful moments worth celebrating. The stories shared on these pages, and your stories highlight the strength and resilience that come from these bonds. They remind us that we are not alone on this path.

And let's not forget the core of our discussion: the immense joy and profound love that define LGBTQ+ parenting. Each narrative we've explored, each piece of advice shared, underscores the fulfillment that comes from parenting— challenges and all. These stories aren't just tales; they affirm the vibrant lives we are building.

As we close this chapter (literally and figuratively), remember that this book isn't the end of your journey. It's a companion for the road ahead, a starting point for deeper exploration and engagement. Keep seeking resources, connecting with your community, and advocating for your family and the LGBTQ+ community.

Now, a call to action for us all: Let's use what we've learned and the stories we've shared to advocate for change. Support LGBTQ+ organizations, participate in community dialogues, and maybe share your story. Each action builds a more inclusive society.

I want to express my gratitude for walking with me through these pages. Your engagement, stories, and challenges inspire a continuing dialogue that enriches us all. We are in this together —today, tomorrow, and all the days to come.

Finally, remember: LGBTQ+ parenting is a journey marked by unique challenges but also unparalleled joy and love. This book serves as a guide, advocate, and companion on that journey, empowering families with knowledge, community, and a voice for advocacy.

Thank you for sharing this part of your journey with me. With love, resilience, and pride, here's to continuing the adventure.

Alex Harper

Now that you have everything you need to raise your children confidently as proud LGBTQ+ parents, it's time to share your newfound knowledge and show other readers where they can find the same support.

Leaving your honest opinion of this book on Amazon will help other LGBTQ+ parents find the guidance they need to navigate their parenting journey with confidence and pride.

Scan the QR code to leave your review on Amazon.

Let's keep pride alive, pass on the torch of knowledge, and support future LGBTQ+ parents. Your role in this journey is crucial, and I am profoundly grateful for your help in making LGBTQ+ parenting more accessible and celebrated.

Here's to continuing our journey with new knowledge and a

shared purpose. Thank you for being an essential part of this adventure.

References

- *LGBTQ+ Family Building Options* https://resolve.org/learn/what-are-my-options/lgbtq-family-building-options/
- *Legal Basics for L.G.B.T.Q. Parents* https://www.nytimes.com/article/legal-basics-for-lgbtq-parents.html
- *LGBTQIA+ Financial Guide to Becoming a Parent* https://www.moneygeek.com/financial-planning/resources/lgbtq-family-costs/
- *PFLAG: Homepage* https://pflag.org/
- *Penn LGBTQ Family Building Program* https://www.pennmedicine.org/for-patients-and-visitors/find-a-program-or-service/penn-fertility-care/lgbtq-family-building
- *How Do You Protect Your Parental Rights in LGBT Surrogacy?* https://surrogate.com/intended-parents/surrogacy-for-lgbt-parents/parental-rights-in-lgbt-surrogacy/#:~:text=One%20of%20the%20most%20common,after%20your%20child%20is%20born.
- *Same-sex adoption in the United States* https://en.wikipedia.org/wiki/Same-sex_adoption_in_the_United_States
- *Fertility preservation options for transgender individuals* https://www.ncbi.nlm.nih.gov/pmc/articles/PMC7108981/
- *Legal Basics for L.G.B.T.Q. Parents* https://www.nytimes.com/article/legal-basics-for-lgbtq-parents.html
- *A Pediatrician's Guide to an LGBTQ+ Friendly Practice - AAP* https://www.aap.org/en/patient-care/lgbtq-health-and-wellness/a-pediatricians-guide-to-an-lgbtq-friendly-practice/#:~:text=Provide%20patient%20education%20materials%20that,pronouns%20shows%20understanding%20and%20acceptance.
- *How Do Microaggressions Affect the LGBTQ+ Community?* https://healthmatters.nyp.org/how-microaggressions-affect-the-lgbtq-community/
- *Family Equality - Advancing Equality for LGBTQ Families* https://familyequality.org/
- *Why is LGBTQI+ inclusive education so important and what ...*

https://www.sddirect.org.uk/blog-article/why-lgbtqi-inclusive-education-so-important-and-what-can-be-done

- *Creating Safe & Inclusive Schools for LGBTQ Families* https://familyequality.org/wp-content/uploads/2018/08/toolkit-safeschoolsv2.pdf
- *PFLAG: Homepage* https://pflag.org/
- *LGBT Parents and Social Media: Advocacy, Privacy, and …* https://yardi.people.si.umich.edu/pubs/Schoenebeck_LGBTParents16.pdf
- *Resources for Creating LGBTQ-Inclusive Schools* https://www.hrc.org/news/resources-for-creating-lgbtq-inclusive-schools
- *These Approaches Can Prevent Bullying in School* https://www.glsen.org/blog/these-approaches-can-prevent-bullying-school
- *A Guide to Your Legal Rights as an LGBTQ+ Parent* https://www.thebump.com/a/lgbtq-parental-rights
- *How to Help Teens with Gender Identity* https://www.bgca.org/news-stories/2022/March/how-to-help-teens-with-gender-identity
- *How Parental Support Affects Mental Health of LGBTQ Youth* https://www.healthline.com/health-news/how-parental-support-affects-mental-health-of-lgbtq-youth
- *Human Rights Campaign Foundation's 2024 Healthcare Equality Index Reveals Policy Progress and Gaps for LGBTQ+ Inclusion in Healthcare Facilities Nationwide* https://www.hrc.org/press-releases/human-rights-campaign-foundations-2024-healthcare-equality-index-reveals-policy-progress-and-gaps-for-lgbtq-inclusion-in-healthcare-facilities-nationwide
- *Resilience & Mental Health Statistics Among LGBTQ+ Youth* https://www.thetrevorproject.org/research-briefs/resilience-and-mental-health-among-lgbtq-youth-june-2022/
- *Nutrition and Health in the Lesbian, Gay, Bisexual …* https://www.ncbi.nlm.nih.gov/pmc/articles/PMC10721458/
- *State Equality Index 2023* https://www.hrc.org/resources/state-equality-index
- *LGBTQI+ Travel Information* https://travel.state.gov/content/travel/en/international-travel/before-you-go/travelers-with-special-considerations/lgbtqi.html
- *9 Supreme Court Cases That Shaped LGBTQ Rights in America* https://time.com/5694518/lgbtq-supreme-court-cases/
- *Estate Planning Considerations for LGBTQ Couples* https://www.

nolo.com/legal-encyclopedia/six-key-estate-planning-issues-gay-lesbian-couples.html

- *24 LGBTQ+ Couples Share the Story of How They Built ...* https://www.gayparentstobe.com/gay-parenting-blog/lgbtq-parents-share-the-story-of-how-they-built-their-families
- *LGBTQ rights under legal attack around the world* https://www.dw.com/en/lgbtq-rights-worldwide-report-2023/a-66601820
- *Caring for Trans, Nonbinary, and Gender-Expansive ...* https://www.ncbi.nlm.nih.gov/pmc/articles/PMC9679586/
- *PFLAG: Homepage* https://pflag.org/